Latin for Common Entrance

Level 3 and Scholarship

Fred Pragnell

Revised edition June 2013

ISBN 978-0-9573829-2-3

By the same author

A Week in the Middle East An Arabic Language Reader, with CDs 1984,
revised 2003 ISBN 095446062-6

Arabic in Action *A Basic Course in Spoken Arabic* 1992 with CDs ISBN 0-9544606-4-2

London Times EFL course combining grammar with historical themes and the main attractions of
London, 2001 revised and reprinted 2011 ISBN 0-9549538-4-3

The Arab News Arabic-English Reader for Intermediate Students, with CDs 2003
ISBN 0-9544606-0-X

*Palestine Chronicle 1880 – 1950 Extracts from the Arabic press tracing the main political and social
developments* 2005, revised with a set of translations and word list on CD 2008 ISBN 0-9549538-0-0

Preparatory Arabic, *A Basic Course in Arabic for Schools* 2010 ISBN 0-9549538-4-3

The Adventures of Odysseus, A Basic Greek Reader 2012 ISBN 0-9549538-7-8

The Odyssey The Story in Basic Latin 2012 ISBN 0-9549538-8-6

Cambridge Latin Course Conversion Vocabulary 2012 ISBN 0-9549538-6-X

An Introduction to Classical Greek co-authored with Kris Waite, Galore Park 2012
ISBN 9781905735884

Latin for Common Entrance Level 1 2013 ISBN 978-0-9573829-0-9
Latin for Common Entrance Level 2 2013 ISBN 978-0-9573829-1-6
Latin for Common Entrance Levels 1&2 Workbook 2013 ISBN 978-0-9573829-3-0

Series Editor of Translating Arabic Literature:

Modern Iraqi Short Stories 1 Sayyab Books 2009 ISBN 978-1-906228-125
Ten Stories from Iraq 3 Sayyab Books 2011 ISBN 978 1 90 6228 989
The Scent of Winter and other stories by Mahmoud Abdul Wahab Sayyab Books 2012
ISBN 978-1-906228-37-8
The Train Heading up to Baghdad A dual language Arabic-English Reader, based on the short story by
Mahmoud Abdul Wahab, with notes, exercises and CD 2013   ISBN 978-1-906228-47-7

Printed in Great Britain
By **four point printing**

Introduction

This book 3 follows on from and builds upon books 1 and 2 of **Latin for Common Entrance**. Chapters 1 - 12 cover all the vocabulary and grammar needed for CE Level 3 and Chapters 13 - 19 cover the additional constructions for the ISEB and senior schools' scholarship examinations.

The core format is similar to that of the first two books: the new vocabulary and grammar are reinforced by exercises, both from and into Latin. However, in contrast to the first two books, there is no extra material here, like word searches, crosswords or historical or language background. There is a very clear reason for this.

Most senior schools, which start on book 3 of the Cambridge Latin Course, like pupils entering Year 9 to have completed CE level 2, the material covered in the first two books. Whilst the main infantry trudge or meander their way through the level 2 syllabus in years 7 and 8, some pupils, urged on by the glint of Level 3 silver or even by scholarship gold, upgrade to the cavalry and find that they have to cover, perhaps in half a year, constructions that will form the core of the GCSE grammar syllabus - a heady task, but one relished by the cavalrymen of Year 8. To help them on their way, each construction introduced in here is thoroughly treated and embedded into previous learning by the copious sentences both into and from English.

As in books 1 and 2, there are both core and extra exercises. The answers to the Latin-English sentences are to be found at the back of the book. This will allow pupils to work at their own rate and correct the exercises as they complete them. If time is very limited, the extra exercises can be omitted. On the other hand, pupils should be encouraged to attempt all the English sentences as they force recall of the core vocabulary and encourage mastery of the grammar.

Once the material up to the required level has been covered, pupils will be in a position to consolidate their knowledge by tackling some continuous passages. This is necessary to encourage reading fluency and build up confidence to tackle the unseen passages in the examination.

Pupils who do not need to do CE level 3 can prepare for life in the senior school by working their way through my **Cambridge Latin Course Conversion Vocabulary**, which, through a series of carefully graded exercises, with answers, introduces the two hundred words that have appeared in the first two volumes of CLC and that are not on the CE syllabus and at the same time reviews the grammar covered in CE levels 1 and 2.

Pupils who are looking to improve their reading fluency will benefit from **The Odyssey, The Story in Basic Latin.** Written for CE level 2 pupils, the reader introduces a further two hundred words which will be met in the senior school.

I would like to thank Merchant Taylors' School, Hertfordshire for permission to use their scholarship passages and sentences on pages 63 – 65 and my daughter, Karina, for doing the drawings to help enliven the text. The accompanying multiple choice sentences provide scope for improving reading and logic skills.

Fred Pragnell   January 2013

Contents

Chapter 1 The passive voice present tense

So far, the verbs you have met have all been in the active voice. Examples:

The soldier is warning the general. We send the messenger. They throw the arrows. You are punishing the slave.

We can put these sentences into the passive voice thus:

The general is being warned by the soldier. The messenger is sent by us. The arrows are thrown by them. The slave is being punished by you.

Since the passive voice occurs most commonly in the 3rd person singular and plural, it is these that need to be learned and recognised.

1stconj.	2nd conj.	3rd conj.	4th conj.	Mixed conj.
amor	moneor	regor	audior	capior
amaris	moneris	regeris	audiris	caperis
amatur	monetur	regitur	auditur	capitur
amamur	monemur	regimur	audimur	capimur
amamini	monemini	regimini	audimini	capimini
amantur	monentur	reguntur	audiuntur	capiuntur

amor = I am loved, or I am being loved
monemur = we are warned, we are being warned
non reguntur = they are not ruled, they are not being ruled
auditur = (s)he, it is heard, (s)he, it is being heard
capimini = you are taken, you are being taken

Note: The passive of video = I see **videor** = **I seem** or **I appear**

magister iratus esse videtur.
The teacher seems to be angry.

There is **no** present, imperfect or future passive of facio

1 servus miser ab ancilla pulchra spectatur.
2 rex iratus a regina necatur.
3 ancilla pulchra ab agricola laeto spectatur.
4 ancilla laeta a sene sapienti laudatur.
5 femina crudelis a filio audaci auditor.

Exercise 1.1   Translate into English, giving just one version

1. amantur   2. moneris   3. regitur   4. non audimur   5. non caperis

Exercise 1.1E Translate into English, giving just one version

1. amatur   2. monemini 3. regeris   4. non audiuntur   5. non capimini

Exercise 1.2   Translate into Latin

1. He is loved
2. They are warned
3. We are ruled
4. They are being heard
5. She is captured

Exercise 1.2E   Translate into Latin

1. They are loved
2. He isn't warned
3. You *(sing.)* are ruled
4. We are being heard
5. We are captured

1 murus ingens a sene misero lente deletur.
2 villa parva ab uxore laeta celeriter aedificatur.
3 corpus magnum ab agricola subito ostenditur.
4 murus parvus a servo iam aedificatur.
5 templum parvum a duce tandem invenitur.

Review of transitive verbs

Exercise 1.3   Translate the following verbs into English

accipio, aedifico, bibo, colligo, conspicio, constituo, consumo, defendo, deleo, duco, expecto, gero, iacio, invenio, iubeo, laudo, lego, libero, mitto, moveo, narro, neco, nuntio, occido, occupo, oppugno, ostendo, paro, pono, porto, reduco, servo, specto, supero, teneo, terreo, trado, voco, vulnero

Exercise 1.4   Translate the following verbs into English

accipiunt, aedificat, bibit, colligunt, conspicit, constituit, consumit, defendunt, delent, ducunt, gerit, iaciunt, invenit, iubent, laudat, legit, liberamus, mittimus, moves, necant, occidit, occupat, oppugnat, ostendit, parat, ponunt, portamus, reducit, servatis, spectant, superas, tenes, terret, tradit, vocat, vulneratis

Exercise 1.5   Put the verbs in Exercise 1.4 into the passive

Exercise 1.6   Translate into Latin

1. it is being built
2. they are defended
3. it is not being destroyed
4. we are being led
5. they are thrown
6. she is praised
7. you *(sing.)* are being sent
8. they are moved
9. it is killed

Exercise 1.6E   Translate into Latin

1. they are occupied
2. it is attacked
3. they are shown
4. it is put
5. they are being carried
6. you *(pl.)* are led back
7. he is overcome
8. she is handed over
9. they are wounded

To translate **by** + a person we use a/ab + ablative

urbs ab hostibus oppugnatur.   The city is being attacked by the enemy.

2

To translate **by** + a thing we use ablative only

urbs hastis oppugnatur.   The city is being attacked by spears.

New vocabulary

interea = meanwhile, in the meantime
lente = slowly
nec …. nec / neque … neque = neither … nor
paene = nearly, almost
superbus -a -um = proud, arrogant
telum -i 2 n. = weapon, missile, spear, javelin

Exercise 1.7   Translate into English

1. hi pueri miseri telis saevis vulnerantur.
2. paene omnes discipuli a magistro superbo laudantur.
3. paene omnes libri a paucis pueris leguntur.
4. interea ceterae naves ventis saevis delentur.
5. pauci servi a domino malo saepe puniuntur.
6. hoc vinum optimum a nautis novis lente bibitur.
7. nautae Graeci a militibus Romanis vincuntur.
8. ille equus dormire videtur.
9. illi hostes fessi telis Romanorum occiduntur.
10. nos a militibus iratis nec capimur nec vulneramur.

Exercise 1.7E   Translate into English

1. Helena pulcherrima a Paride capitur.
2. haec urbs magna a Troianis fortiter defenditur.
3. hi viri fortes a Graecis nec occiduntur nec vulnerantur.
4. hic equus ingens a Graecis validis aedificatur.
5. Helena miserrima a Menelai fortissimo tandem liberatur.
6. Troiani fessi ab his Graecis validissimis facile superantur.
7. multum auri ab illis Graecis felicibus capitur.
8. omnes naves Graecorum discedere videntur.
9. post proelium multum vini a Graecis fessis consumitur.
10. paene omnia tela ab hostibus crudelibus iaciuntur.

Exercise 1.8   Rewrite Exercise 1.7 putting the verbs into the active voice

Exercise 1.8 E Rewrite Exercise 1.7 E putting the verbs into the active voice

Exercise 1.9 Translate into Latin

1. Those huge walls are being defended for a long time by the Trojans.
2. That bad pupil is always punished by the angry teacher.
3. The new ship is being destroyed by the fierce winds.
4. That wine is always drunk by the master.
5. The soldiers are neither killed nor injured by the Romans.
6. This very good book is being read by the wise teacher.
7. A few horses are wounded by the naughty boys.
8. Almost all the soldiers are being wounded in the fierce battle.
9. This arrogant king is being warned by his slaves.
10. These pupils are never praised by the miserable teacher.

Exercise 1.9 E Translate into Latin

1. This large city is being destroyed by the Greeks.
2. Those good pupils are never punished by the teacher.
3. That small town is being attacked by the enemy for a second time.
4. The best food is taken by the angry king.
5. The rest of the soldiers are wounded by the cruel Greeks.
6. Meanwhile this very good wine is being drunk by the teacher.
7. The rest of the young men are being led back by the soldiers.
8. These brave soldiers are being killed by new weapons.
9. That wretched leader is not being warned by his soldiers.
10. This proud old man is being slowly led to the villa by his companion.

1 hastae ab uxoribus saevis iaciuntur.
2 tela magna a nautis crudelibus tenentur.
3 sagittae magnae ab uxoribus saevis delentur.
4 tela parva ab ancillis iaciuntur.
5 hastae a patre et filio tenentur.

1 nauta puellam parvam timet.
2 puella audax nautam terret.
3 femina a nauta pulchro terretur.
4 ancilla superba a sene crudeli terretur.
5 puella parva a nauta saevo terretur

4

Chapter 2 The passive voice imperfect tense

The imperfect passive is translated by 'used to be' or 'was/were being'

1st	2nd	3rd	4th	Mixed
amabar	monebar	regebar	audiebar	capiebar
amabaris	monebaris	regebaris	audiebaris	capiebaris
amabatur	monebatur	regebatur	audiebatur	capiebatur
amabamur	monebamur	regebamur	audiebamur	capiebamur
amabamini	monebamini	regebamini	audiebamini	capiebamini
amabantur	monebantur	regebantur	audiebantur	capiebantur

Thus   amabar = I used to be loved / I was being loved
monebar = I used to be warned / I was being warned
regebar = I used to be ruled / I was being ruled
audiebar = I used to be heard / I was being heard
capiebar = I used to be taken / I was being taken

Exercise 2.1   Translate the following verbs into English using either *was /were being* or *used to be*

accipiebantur, aedificabatur, bibebatur, colligebantur, conspiciebantur, constituebatur, consumebatur, defendebantur, delebantur, ducebatur, gerebatur, iaciebantur, inveniebatur, iubebantur, laudabatur, legebatur, liberabamur, mittebamur, movebaris, necabantur, occidebatur, occupabatur, oppugnabatur, ostendebatur, parabatur, ponebantur, portabamur, reducebatur, servabamini, spectabantur, superabaris, tenebaris, terrebaris, tradebatur, vocabatur, vulnerabantur

1 servus crudelis ab ancilla misera spectabatur.
2 rex iratus a regina tristi necabatur.
3 mater pulchra ab agricola laeto spectabatur
4 ancilla laeta a sene sapienti laudabatur
5 femina crudelis a filio audaci vulnerabatur

Exercise 2.1E Translate the following verbs into English using either *was /were being* or *used to be*

accipiebatur, aedificabatur, bibebantur, colligebamini, conspiciebaris, constituebantur, consumebantur, defendebaris, delebatur, ducebar, gerebantur, iaciebatur, inveniebar, iubebamini, laudabar, legebantur, liberabar, mittebamini, movebamini, necabatur, occidebantur, occupabantur, oppugnabantur, ostendebantur, parabantur, ponebar, portabamini, reducebar, servabantur, spectabatur, superabamini, tenebamini, terrebamini, tradebantur, vocabar, vulnerabatur

Exercise 2.2   Translate into English

1. Helena pulcherrima a Paride capiebatur.
2. urbs parva ab omnibus civibus fortiter defendebatur.

1 aqua a senibus tristibus bibebatur.
2 vinum sacrum ab uxoribus bibebatur.
3 vinum optimum a nautis bibebatur.
4 a senibus aqua diu bibebatur.
5 a patre et filio vinum regi tradebatur.

3. milites Romani ab hostibus fessis non vincebantur.
4. interea equus ingens ab Graecis aedificabatur.
5. uxor felix a coniuge forti tandem liberabatur.
6. Troiani a Graecis audacibus vincebantur.
7. multum vini a Graecis felicibus capiebatur.
8. terra a nautis laetis tandem conspiciebatur.
9. post proelium hic cibus a militibus nostris consumebatur.
10. multa tela ab hostibus saevissimis iaciebantur.

Exercise 2.2E Translate into English

1. servus laborare videbatur.
2. omnes discipuli a magistris sapientibus laudabantur.
3. paene omnes libri ab omnibus pueris legebantur.
4. ceterae naves vento saevo delebantur.
5. pauci servi a regina mala saepe puniebantur.
6. optimum vinum a nautis semper bibebatur.
7. nautae Graeci a militibus audacibus vincebantur.
8. equus miser a servis malis vulnerabatur.
9. omnes hostes a militibus crudelibus gladiis occidebantur.
10. servi a domino nobili et superbo nec puniebantur nec laudabantur.

1 aqua ab ancilla portabatur.
2 vinum a matre bibebatur.
3 aqua a domino portabatur.
4 ancilla a servo malo spectabatur.
5 vinum optimum a custode tradebatur.

Exercise 2.3   Translate into Latin

1. The large city was being destroyed by those cruel Greeks.
2. These bad pupils often used to be punished by the savage teacher.
3. The small towns were being destroyed by the cruel enemy.
4. The best food used to be taken by the wretched king.
5. The rest of the soldiers were being wounded by the Greeks.
6. Wine was often drunk after the meal by all the companions of the leader.
7. The rest of the young men were being led back by those soldiers.
8. Almost all the brave soldiers were being killed by spears and arrows of the enemy.
9. The wretched leader was not being warned by his frightened soldiers.
10. This sad old man was being led to the country-house by his companion.

Exercise 2.3E Translate into Latin

1 nauta saevus puellam parvam timebat.
2 puella crudelis nautam terrebat.
3 femina a comite pulchro terrebatur.
4 mulier superba a sene crudeli terrebatur.
5 puella perterrita a nauta saevo terrebatur.

1. That huge wall was being defended by the Trojans.
2. This good pupil never used to be punished by the teacher.
3. That huge ship was being slowly destroyed by the fierce wind.
4. That excellent wine was always drunk by the general.
5. The rest of the maids were being praised by the queen.
6. Those very bad books were being read by the naughty pupil.
7. Very many horses were being wounded by the cruel young men.
8. Very few soldiers were being captured in the war.
9. The lucky king was being warned about the danger by his slaves.
10. That pupil was neither praised nor punished by the teachers.

Chapter 3 The passive voice future tense; 5th declension nouns

The future passive is not very common, and is mostly found in the 3rd person

1st	2nd	3rd	4th	Mixed
amabor	monebor	regar	audiar	capiar
amaberis	moneberis	regeris	audieris	capieris
amabitur	monebitur	regetur	audietur	capietur
amabimur	monebimur	regemur	audiemur	capiemur
amabimini	monebimini	regemini	audiemini	capiemini
amabuntur	monebuntur	regentur	audientur	capientur

Thus   amabor = I shall be loved
moneberis = you will be warned
regetur = (s)he, it will be ruled
audiemur = we shall be heard
capiemini = you will be taken

1 tela a senibus crudelibus mox iacientur.
2 hastae a mulieribus laetis tandem tenebuntur.
3 sagittae magnae ab uxoribus iam iacientur.
4 tela magna a nautis mox iacientur.
5 sagittae parvae a pueris audacibus tenebuntur.

Exercise 3.1   Translate the following verbs into English

accipientur, aedificabitur, bibetur, colligetur, conspicientur, constituetur, consumetur, defendetur, delebuntur, ducetur, gerentur, iacientur, invenietur, iubebitur, laudabitur, legetur, liberabimur, mittemur, moveberis, necabuntur, occidetur, occupabitur, oppugnabitur, ostendetur, parabitur, ponentur, portabimur, reducetur, servabimini, spectabuntur, superaberis, teneberis, terreberis, tradetur, vocabitur, vulnerabuntur

Exercise 3.1E   Translate the following verbs into English

accipietur, aedificabuntur, bibentur, colligemini, conspicieris, constituentur, consumentur, defenderis, deletur, ducar, gerentur, iacietur, inveniar, iubebimini, laudabor, legentur, liberabor, mittemini, movebimini, necabitur, occidentur, occupabuntur, oppugnabuntur, ostendentur, parabuntur, ponar, portabimini, reducar, servabuntur, spectabitur, superabimini, tenebimini, terrebimini, tradentur, vocabor, vulnerabitur

Fifth declension nouns

This declension has very few nouns; the most common are **res** = thing, matter f. , **dies** = day m. and **res publica** = the public interest, the republic, the state, often written as one word, **fides** = faith, promise f., **spes** = hope f.

	sing.	pl.
nom.	dies	dies
voc.	dies	dies
acc.	diem	dies
gen.	diei	dierum
dat.	diei	diebus
abl.	die	diebus

	sing.	pl.
nom.	res	res
voc.	res	res
acc.	rem	res
gen.	rei	rerum
dat.	rei	rebus
abl.	re	rebus

	sing.	pl.
nom.	respublica	respublicae
voc.	respublica	respublicae
acc.	rempublicam	respublicas
gen.	reipublicae	rerumpublicarum
dat.	reipublicae	rebuspublicis
abl.	republica	rebuspublicis

Two & three, all cases

	masc.	fem.	neut.	m.&f.	neut.
nom.	duo	duae	duo	tres	tria
acc.	duo,duos	duas	duo	tres	tria
gen.	duorum	duarum	duorum	trium	trium
dat.	duobus	duabus	duobus	tribus	tribus
abl.	duobus	duabus	duobus	tribus	tribus

Time

Periods of time

hora horae 1 f. = hour
dies diei 5 m. = day
nox noctis 3 f. = night
mensis mensis 3 m. = month
annus anni 2 m. = year

1 aquila a phoca ingenti mox occidetur.
2 phoca ab iuvene irato tandem vulnerabitur.
3 equa ab aquila parva mox occidetur.
4 phoca perterrita ab aquila iam monebitur.
5 phoca misera ab aquila mox occidetur.

To express time 'how long' Latin uses the accusative case

Ulixes viginti annos aberat.   Odysseus was away for twenty years.
senex omnem noctem dormivit.   The old man slept all night.

sometimes **per** is put before the accusative of time. Thus,

hostes per multos dies in illo loco manserunt.
The enemy remained in that place for many days

To express time 'when' Latin uses the ablative case

Graeci decimo anno belli equum aedificaverunt.
The Greeks built a horse in the tenth year of the war.

secunda hora discesserunt. They left at the second
hour *(after dawn)*.

The Roman 'day' from dawn to dusk was divided into
twelve equal parts. Hence the length of the 'day' would
depend on season of the year and latitude.

1 tres milites duabus horis redibunt.
2 duo agricolae tres horas ambulaverunt.
3 duo milites tres horas dormiebant.
4 senes in via sedebant.
5 milites oppido iam appropinquant.

To express time 'within which' Latin uses the ablative case

dux tribus horis redibit.   The general will return within three hours.

Place

	in / at	**to / towards**	**from**
normal nouns	in + abl.	ad + acc.	ab / ex + abl.
	in agro	ad agrum	ex agro
cities	'locative'	acc. only	abl. only
	Romae	Romam	Roma
	in Rome	to Rome	from Rome
domus	domi	domum	domo
	at home	to home	from home

Note: domus f. is an irregular noun of 4th declension, to be learnt later
         Prepositions are not used with towns

Exercise 3.2   Translate into English

1. puellae miserae a militibus saevis non vulnerabuntur.
2. paene omnes discipuli a magistris sapientibus cras laudabuntur.
3. illi libri ab omnibus pueris tribus mensibus legentur.
4. ceterae naves tempestate saeva quinque diebus delebuntur.
5. pauci servi a regina mala tertio die punientur.
6. milites per multa horas in oppido manebunt.
7. nautae Graeci a militibus audacibus duabus horis vincentur.

9

8. equi miseri a servis malis capientur.
9. custodes a militibus crudelibus gladiis tribus horis occidentur.
10. servi boni a domino nobili non punientur.

Exercise 3.2E   Translate into English

1. servi Romam duobus diebus reducentur.
2. urbs parva a civibus fortibus duos annos defendetur.
3. milites Romani ab hostibus fessis nec vincentur nec vulnerabuntur.
4. equus ingens a Graecis sex diebus aedificabitur.
5. uxor felix a coniuge forti tribus horis liberabitur.
6. Troiani a Graecis audacibus secunda nocte vincentur.
7. multum auri a Graecis felicibus capietur.
8. insula a nautis laetis cras conspicietur.
9. post proelium omnis cibus a militibus consumetur.
10. multae sagittae a militibus nostris iacientur.

1 miles et femina quinta hora discesserunt.
2 agricola et puella amici sunt.
3 femina et senex iam discesserunt.
4 comes militis et amica cibum consumunt.
5 parentes filii tertia hora redibunt.

Exercise 3.3   Translate into Latin

1. Almost all the huge walls will be destroyed by the enemy within two days.
2. This bad pupil will be punished by the teacher tomorrow.
3. That huge ship will be destroyed by the fierce winds within three months.
4. That excellent wine will be drunk by the old men all night.
5. Those maids will be praised by the queen.
6. Those excellent horses will be captured by the Romans within three days.
7. Very many horses will be wounded in the fierce battle.
8. The bravest soldiers will be killed in the war.
9. The lucky king will soon be warned about the danger by his slaves.
10. That pupil will be praised by all the teachers.

Exercise 3.3E   Translate into Latin

1. This large city will be attacked for three months.
2. These pupils will be often punished by the wretched teacher.
3. The small town will be destroyed by the enemy within ten days.
4. Almost all the best food will be eaten with five days.
5. Very many soldiers will be wounded in the battle tomorrow.
6. Wine will be drunk tomorrow by all the soldiers.
7. The rest of the young men will be led back to town within two hours.
8. These brave soldiers will be killed immediately by the spears and arrows of the enemy.
9. The proud king will soon be warned of the danger of war.
10. This sad old man will be taken back to his villa on the fifth day.

Chapter 4 Two irregular verbs: volo and nolo

volo velle volui = I want

present	imperfect	future	perfect	pluperfect
volo	volebam	volam	volui	volueram
vis	volebas	voles	voluisti	volueras
vult	volebat	volet	voluit	voluerat
volumus	volebamus	volemus	voluimus	volueramus
vultis	volebatis	voletis	voluistis	volueratis
volunt	volebant	volent	voluerunt	voluerant

nolo nolle nolui = I don't want

present	imperfect	future	perfect	pluperfect
nolo	nolebam	nolam	nolui	nolueram
non vis	nolebas	noles	noluisti	nolueras
non vult	nolebat	nolet	noluit	noluerat
nolumus	nolebamus	nolemus	noluimus	nolueramus
non vultis	nolebatis	noletis	noluistis	nolueratis
nolunt	nolebant	nolent	noluerunt	noluerant

Like **possum**, these two verbs are often followed by the infinitive

discedere volunt. They want to leave.

discipuli scribere nolebant.   The pupils were not wanting to write.

Exercise 4.1   Translate into English

1. accipere vult
2. aedificare volunt
3. bibere volebat
4. colligere volui
5. consumere volueramus
6. defendere voluimus
7. delere non vis
8. ducere nolebant
9. exspectare nolemus
10. gerere nolueratis
11. iacere vult
12. invenire volebat
13. iubere nolumus
14. laudare vultis
15. legerene vis?
16. liberarene eos vultis?
17. mittere noluerunt
18. movere volent
19. narrare nolent
20. necare volet
21. nuntiare volumus
22. occidere volet
23. occupare voluistis
24. oppugnare nolo
25. ostendere noluimus
26. parare non vult
27. ponere nolebant
28. portare noluit
29. reducere nolebatis
30. servarene vis?
31. spectarene vultis?
32. superare voluit
33. tenere volebat
34. terrere nolo
35. tradere nolent
36. vocare vultis

Exercise 4.1E Translate into English

1. accipere volam	2. aedificare voluerunt	3. bibere volebamus
4. colligere voluerunt	5. consumere volueram	6. defendere voluistis
7. delere non vultis	8. ducere volebant	9. exspectare volemus
10. gerere noluimus	11. iacere volebant	12. invenire volebant
13. iubere volumus	14. laudare vult	15. legerene vultis?
16. liberarene eam volunt?	17. mittere nolet	18. movere voletis
19. narrare nolunt	20. necare voluerunt	21. nuntiare volo
22. occidere volent	23. occupare voluisti	24. oppugnare non vis
25. ostendere noluerunt	26. parare nolemus	27. ponere nolebat
28. portare nolebamus	29. reducere nolebant	30. servarene volunt?
31. spectarene vis?	32. superare voluerunt	33. tenere volebant
34. terrere volo	35. tradere noluerat	36. vocare voluerunt

New Nouns

somnus -i 2 m. = sleep
praemium -i 2 n. = prize, reward

animal animalis 3 n. = animal *(see box)*
custos custodis 3 c. = guard
gens gentis 3 f. = race, tribe
labor laboris 3 m. = task, work
opus operis 3 n. = work, task
princeps principis 3 m. = chief, prince, emperor
tempestas tempestatis 3 f. = storm

Sing.	
n.v.acc.	animal
gen.	animalis
dat.abl.	animali
Pl.	
n.v.acc.	animalia
gen.	animalium
dat.abl.	animalibus

Exercise 4.2 Translate into English

1. post proelium princeps fessus dormire volebat.
2. omnia animalia tempestate saeva occidentur.
3. omnes gens spem in principe ponere volebant.
4. omnes gentes Graeciae cum Troianis pugnare voluerunt.
5. Romani rempublicam diu bene gesserunt.
6. nos labore omnium civium hostes superare potuimus.
7. servi, quamquam opus difficile erat, multas horas bene laboraverunt.
8. 'fidem mihi habete, o milites!' clamavit dux.
9. milites, quamquam multum vini biberant, somnum capere non potuerunt.
10. gentes Britanniae inter se saepe pugnabant.

1 aquila equam spectare vult.
2 phoca misera fugere nolebat.
3 aquila saeva comitem occidere voluit.
4 aquila magna phocam occidere vult.
5 phoca fortis effugere noluit.

Exercise 4.2E   Translate into English

1. ante proelium princeps omnem spem victoriae habebat.
2. Quintus iuvenis magnae spei est.
3. Romani fidem reipublicae diu habebant.
4. gentes fidem principi forti posuerunt.
5. tres custodes ante murum vinum bibebant.
6. nos in duce valido omnes spes ponimus.
7. milites animalia servare spem semper habuerunt.
8. omnem spem hostes vincere habemus.
9. senex, quod opus longum et difficile est, mox somno capietur.
10. hostes vincere erit res magni laboris.

1 nauta miser discedere volebat.
2 femina et miles cantare voluerunt.
3 nauta laetus cum femina pulchra sedere vult.
4 magister perterritus domum ire vult.
5 nauta reginam de periculo monere voluit.

Exercise 4.3 Translate into Latin

1. Before the battle few soldiers were wanting to fight.
2. Because he had drunk a lot of wine, the general's companion was not wanting to leave.
3. O emperor, why do you want to kill these animals?
4. The enemy does not want to hand over the young men.
5. The lazy boys will not want to do these difficult tasks.
6. Three wild tribes wandered in Italy for a long time.
7. Have faith in these new guards, o general!
8. We didn't want to put hope in the new leader.
9. After we had taken the prizes, we were unwilling to leave at once.
10. The sailors were unwilling to sail in the wild storm.

1 pueri libros legere volebant.
2 magister laetus dormire vult.
3 tres senes scribere nolebant.
4 magister parvus discipulos punire volebat.
5 discipuli scribere nolebant.

Exercise 4.3 E Translate into Latin

1. After the battle, the three guards ran away.
2. Who wants to drink this excellent wine?
3. These brave soldiers took all the prizes.
4. What do you want to do now, young man?
5. I don't want to sail in this fierce storm.
6. Suddenly the fierce animals rushed down the street.
7. Put your trust in this new leader, o citizens!
8. All these tasks are very difficult for me.
9. Although the enemy was attacking the town, the citizens were unwilling to run away.
10. Guards, capture those animals at once!

1 miles felix puellam parvam terrere volebat.
2 nauta saevus puellam terrere vult.
3 senex malus feminam tristem ducere voluit.
4 dux fortis comitem laetam occidere volebat.
5 princeps de periculo uxorem volebat.

Chapter 5 Perfect passive tense

To correspond to the perfect tense active *I warned, I have warned, I did warn* **monui**, we have the perfect tense passive *I was warned, I have been warned.*

The perfect tense passive in Latin is made up of two parts:

The first part is the **perfect participle passive** and the second part is the **present tense** of the verb **sum** to be (sum, es, est, sumus, estis, sunt)

The **perfect participle passive** is formed from the **supine** of the verb. Up to now we have had no need for the supine. However, when you look up a verb in a dictionary you will normally find four principal parts. For example:

amo 1st pers. sing. pres. **-are** infinitive **-avi** 1st pers. sing. perfect **-atum** supine 1st conjug.

All verbs in the 1st conjugation follow this pattern. Thus,

| clamo | clamare | clamavi | clamatum |
| voco | vocare | vocavi | vocatum |

even

| do | dare | dedi | datum |
| sto | stare | steti | statum |

1 equa laeta ab aquila conspecta est.
2 aquila a phoca iam vulnerata est.
3 animal a phoca tandem conspectum est.
4 custos tamen a phoca occisus est.
5 phoca ab aquila iam conspecta est.

You may have noticed that taking off the **-um** and adding **-ion** will often give us an English word. (ex)clamation, vocation, station

However the supines of the 2nd, 3rd and mixed conjugation verbs need to be learnt. For ease of learning and reference, the principal parts of all the verbs met so far are listed below

accipio	ĕre	accepi	acceptum	3½	receive
audio	ire	audivi	auditum	4	hear, listen to
bibo	ĕre	bibi	bibitum	3	drink
capio	ĕre	cepi	captum	3½	take, capture
colligo	ĕre	collegi	collectum	3	collect
conspicio	ĕre	conspexi	conspectum	3½	catch sight of
constituo	ĕre	constitui	constitutum	3	decide
consumo	ĕre	consumpsi	consumptum	3	eat
cupio	ĕre	cupivi	cupitum	3½	want
curro	ĕre	cucurri	cursum	3	run
defendo	ĕre	defendi	defensum	3	defend
deleo	ēre	delevi	deletum	2	destroy
dico	ĕre	dixi	dictum	3	say, tell

discedo	ĕre	discessi	discessum	3	depart
dormio	ire	dormivi	dormitum	4	sleep
duco	ĕre	duxi	ductum	3	lead
eo	ire	ii	itum		go
effugio	ĕre	effugi	-	3½	escape
exeo	ire	exii	exitum		go out
facio	ĕre	feci	factum	3½	make, do
fugio	ĕre	fugi	fugitum	3½	flee
gero	ĕre	gessi	gestum	3	carry on, do, wage
iacio	ĕre	ieci	iactum	3½	throw
ineo	ire	inii	initum		enter
invenio	ire	inveni	inventum	4	find, discover
iubeo	ēre	iussi	iussum	2	order
lego	ĕre	legi	lectum	3	read, choose
ludo	ĕre	lusi	lusum	3	play
maneo	ēre	mansi	mansum	2	remain
mitto	ĕre	misi	missum	3	send
moveo	ēre	movi	motum	2	move
occido	ĕre	occidi	occisum	3	kill
ostendo	ĕre	ostendi	ostentum	3	show
pereo	ĕre	perii	peritum		perish, die
pono	ĕre	posui	positum	3	put
redeo	ire	redii	reditum		return
reduco	ĕre	reduxi	reductum	3	led back
rego	ĕre	rexi	rectum	3	rule
respondeo	ēre	respondi	responsum	2	answer
rideo	ēre	risi	risum	2	laugh
ruo	ĕre	rui	rutum	3	rush, collapse, charge
scribo	ĕre	scripsi	scriptum	3	write
teneo	ēre	tenui	tentum	2	hold
terreo	ēre	terrui	territum	2	frighten
timeo	ēre	timui	-	2	fear
trado	ĕre	tradidi	traditum	3	hand over
transeo	ire	transii	transitum		cross
video	ēre	visi	visum	2	see

Exercise 5.1

Write down English words that come from the supines by taking off **-um** and adding **-ion**. Some come with a prefix at the beginning of the English word.

It is useful to learn the principal parts of any new verb met.

To form the **past participle passive, PPP**, take off the **-um** from the supine and add
-us -a -um

So from **monitum**, the supine of moneo, we get
monitus monita monitum, the past participle passive.

The final stage is to put it with the verb **sum** to be

monitus sum   = I was warned, I have been warned

Of course, because the PPP functions as an adjective,
if the speaker is female, this will be **monita sum**.
Similarly, **moniti sumus** or **monitae sumus** =
we were / have been warned.

1 femina a comite audaci territa est.
2 nauta fortis a puella tristi territus est.
3 mater a filio saevo punita est.
4 puella misera a nauta crudeli territa est.
5 uxor sapiens a nauta de periculo monita est.

So the full table will be:

	masculine	feminine	neuter
singular	-us	-a	-um
plural	-i	-ae	-a

Examples:

servus captus est.	The slave was / has been captured.
puellae monitae sunt.	The girls were/ have been warned.
oppidum inventum est.	The town was / has been discovered.

Exercise 5.2   Translate into English

1. praemia tertio die accepta sunt.
2. vox pulchra mulieris ab iuvene audita est.
3. hastae ducis a servo captae sunt.
4. ceteri servi in medio oppido iam collecti sunt.
5. puer a patre conspectus est.
6. bellum a rege constitutum est.
7. cibus a militibus heri consumptus est.
8. oppidum a civibus diu defensum est.
9. muri ab iuvenibus deleti sunt.
10. haec verba a rege dicta sunt.
11. illa animalia ad agrum ducta sunt.
12. aqua ab ancilla iam bibita est.
13. illae res celeriter gestae sunt.
14. paucae sagittae in oppidum iacta sunt.
15. hoc aurum Romae inventum est .
16. hic miles discedere iussus est.
17. dux pessimus a rege lectus est.
18. undeviginti milites ad urbem missi sunt.
19. equi quarta hora moti sunt.
20. servus miser secunda hora occisus est.
21. praemia ibi heri posita sunt.
22. cetera animalia Romam reducta sunt.
23. Romani diu a regibus recti sunt.
24. parva pars libri a tribus discipulis scripta est.
25. omnes libri a discipulo traditi sunt.
26. ille iuvenis Romae heri visus est.

Exercise 5.2E   Translate into English

1. praemium secundo anno acceptum est.
2. aqua celeriter ab equo bibita est.
3. omnes hastae ab iuvene captae sunt.
4. milites a duce iam collecti sunt.
5. nos a magistro conspecti sumus.
6. bellum a principe tandem constitutum est.
7. cibus ab equo iam consumptus est.
8. urbs a civibus fortiter defensa est.
9. villa pulcherrima a custodibus deleta est.
10. haec verba a duce tristi dicta sunt.
11. illi milites Romam ducti sunt.
12. homo factus est.
13. hae res bene gestae sunt.
14. omnes hastae in hostes iam iactae sunt.
15. hoc aurum sub villa inventum est.
16. hoc miles discedere iussus est.
17. dux optimus a militibus lectus est.
18. septem custodes ad mare missi sunt.
19. arma heri a puero audaci mota sunt.
20. princeps tertia hora occisus est.
21. aurum ibi heri positum est.
22. milites ad flumen reducti sunt.
23. Roma diu a regibus recta est.
24. hic liber a poeta claro scriptus est.
25. servi miseri a domino traditi sunt.
26. omnia animalia in agro heri visa sunt.

Exercise 5.3   Translate into Latin

1. All the weapons were taken by the young men.
2. The rest of the soldiers were collected into the centre of the city.
3. The voice of the little girl was not heard by her mother.
4. Many large towns were destroyed by the enemy.
5. Those bad words were not said by our noble and wise leader.
6. The chieftain of this tribe was killed in the battle yesterday.
7. A part of this book was written by the king.
8. All the soldiers were led back to Rome immediately.
9. Our books were handed over to the teacher yesterday.
10. Our town was defended for two years by the brave citizens.

1 mater laeta a filio et filia laudata est.
2 puer et puella a matre dormire iussi sunt.
3 mater iratissima est.
4 puer et puella legere volebant.
5 uxor coniugem et filiam spectabat.

Exercise 5.3E   Translate into Latin

1. All the books were taken by our teacher.
2. A few slaves were sent to the field yesterday.
3. The beautiful voice of the woman was heard by all the citizens.
4. All the country-houses were destroyed by the fierce storm.
5. These bad words were said by that young man.
6. The general was killed by a spear in the battle.
7. A large part of the book was written by a Greek slave.
8. These young men were led back to the city.
9. The book was handed over to the king.
10. Our city was defended for three years by the brave soldiers.

1 villa a servo deleta est.
2 murus ab uxore statim aedificatus est.
3 servus in tempestate vulneratus est.
4 templum a servo caro aedificatum est.
5 murus in agro aedificatus est.

Chapter 6 Pluperfect passive tense

The **pluperfect passive** tense is formed by the **perfect passive participle** + the imperfect tense of sum:

servus captus erat.   The slave had been captured.
puellae monitae erant.   The girls had been warned.
oppidum inventum erat.   The town had been discovered.

Exercise 6.1   Translate into English

1. praemia quarto anno accepta erant.
2. vox iuvenis a puella audita erat.
3. arma principis a servo capta erant.
4. omnes servi in urbe iam collecti erant.
5. puer a matre iam conspectus erat.
6. bellum a principe constitutum erat.
7. cibus ab equis heri consumptus erat.
8. muri a civibus diu defensi erant.
9. muri urbis ab hostibus deleti erant.
10. haec verba mala a rege dicta erant.
11. illud animal ad agrum ductum erat.
12. vinum a regina iam bibitum erat.
13. hae res tandem gestae erant.
14. plurimae sagittae in oppidum iacta erant.
15. omne aurum in villa inventum erat.
16. hic iuvenis discedere iussus erat.
17. dux sapiens a principe lectus erat.
18. undeviginti milites Romam missi erant.

Exercise 6.1E   Translate into English

1. equus quinta hora motus erat.
2. princeps secunda hora occisus erat.
3. omnia praemia hic heri posita erant.
4. cetera animalia domum reducta erant.
5. Britanni diu a Romanis recti erant.
6. hic liber a poeta claro scriptus erat.
7. omnes servi a duce traditi erant.
8. comes meus in oppido heri visus erat.

New Verbs

cogo	ĕre	coegi	coactum	3	drive, force *(+ acc. and infin.)*
contendo	ĕre	contendi	contentum	3	hurry, march
convenio	ire	conveni	conventum	4	meet
credo	ĕre	credidi	-	3	believe, trust *(+dat.)*
custodio	ire	custodivi	custoditum	4	guard
interficio	ĕre	interfeci	interfectum	3½	kill
iuvo	are	iuvi	iutum	1	help
pello	ĕre	pepuli	pulsum	3	drive
peto	ĕre	petivi	petitum	3	look for, seek, attack
relinquo	ĕre	reliqui	relictum	3	leave

Exercise 6.2   Translate into English

1. agricolae animalia in agrum currere cogunt.
2. milites muros diu custodiunt.
3. ego amicos semper iuvo.
4. miles principem interficit.
5. venti saevi navem pellunt.
6. agricola miser animalia petit.
7. pater filium domo relinquit.

Exercise 6.2E Translate into English

1. agricola filium domo manere cogit.
2. custodes fessi muros custodiunt.
3. princeps uxorem semper iuvat.
4. milites servum interficiunt.
5. tempestates saevae naves pellunt.
6. servi miseri animal petunt.
7. duces milites in urbe relinquunt.

1 puella laeta a nauta crudeli iam territa erat.
2 nauta tristis ab uxore superba tandem territa erat.
3 coniunx misera a nuntio malo monita erat.
4 puella a nauta nono territa erat.
5 puella quarta a sene pessimo vulnerata erat.

Exercise 6.3   Put the sentences in Ex 6.2E
into the passive without translating

Exercise 6.3E Put the sentences in Ex 6.2
into the passive without translating

Exercise 6.4   Change the verbs in Ex. 6.2
from the present to the perfect tense

Exercise 6.4E Change the verbs in Ex. 6.2E
from the present to the perfect tense

Exercise 6.5   Translate into English

1. animalia a servo cibum malum consumere coacta sunt.
2. omnes iuvenes in media urbe convenerunt.
3. uxor a principe iuta erat.
4. servus a militibus interfectus est.
5. naves tempestate saeva pulsae erant.
6. animal a servis miseris petitum erat.
7. milites in urbe a duce relicti sunt.
8. milites duci sapienti credit.
9. iuvenes ad urbem contendebant.
10. muri a custodibus custoditi erant.

1 aqua a sene statim lata erat.
2 omne vinum a muliere bibitum erat.
3 vinum ad villam ab ancilla latum erat.
4 ancilla domum a coniuge reducta erat.
5 filia regis Romam cum fratre missa erat.

Exercise 6.5E Translate into English

1. cives miseri ab hostibus ex urbe fugere coacti erant.
2. muri ab iuvenibus custoditi sunt.
3. coniunx ab uxore iutus est.
4. servus ab hostibus interfectus erat.
5. navis tempestate saeva pulsa est.
6. animal ab servis petitum est.
7. mulieres in urbe a militibus relictae erant.
8. ego amicis semper credo.
9. senes in villa cras convenient.
10. milites ad flumen celeriter contenderunt.

Exercise 6.6 Translate into Latin

1. The father hurried to the city with his wife.
2. The animals were driven to the fields by the old man.
3. We always trust our general.
4. The walls were being guarded by the tired soldiers.
5. All the enemy soldiers were killed in the battle.
6. 'Help me, father!' shouted the boy.
7. All the ships had been driven across the sea by the fierce storm.
8. The sad old man was looking for his animals.
9. We left the slaves at home and escaped.
10. With the help of our allies we drove the enemy from the town.

1 puella tristis a patre crudeli iam punita erat.
2 senex miser a filia irata punitus erat.
3 uxor fessa a coniuge sapienti non punita erat.
4 regina laeta in via a militibus non conspecta erat.
5 puella laeta a patre laudata erat.

Exercise 6.6E Translate into Latin

1. The girl's mother will hurry to the river with her husband.
2. The young men will not drive the animals into the river.
3. We never used to trust that evil man.
4. 'Guard the prizes, boys!' shouted the teacher.
5. By chance a soldier killed the old man with his sword.
6. The boy's father always helped his son.
7. All the ships had been driven across the sea by
   the fierce storm.
8. The son will look for his father in the centre of the town.
9. The leader had left the soldiers in the town.
10. With the help of these soldiers we'll drive the enemy
    from the city.

1 agricolae tempestate territi erant.
2 senes mali ab aquilis ferocibus conspecti erant.
3 socii vento saevo ad insulam pulsi erant.
4 nautae miseri ab aquilis petiti erant.
5 nautae undis altis territi erant.

Chapter 7 fero, totus, relative clauses

fero

The verb **fero** = **I carry, bring** has some irregular forms.

The principal parts of **fero** are   **fero   ferre   tuli   latum**

Note that the English words *translation* and *transfer* come from different parts of the same verb **fero**.

When we bring help to someone Latin uses the dative. Thus,

auxilium meis amicis semper fero.
I always bring help to my friends.

active	present	imperfect	future	perfect	pluperfect
	fero	ferebam	feram	tuli	tuleram
	fers	ferebas	feres	tulisti	tuleras
	fert	ferebat	feret	tulit	tulerat
	ferimus	ferebamus	feremus	tulimus	tuleramus
	fertis	ferebatis	feretis	tulistis	tuleratis
	ferunt	ferebant	ferent	tulerunt	tulerant

infinitive ferre **imperative sing.** fer **pl.** ferte

passive	present	imperfect	future	perfect	pluperfect
	feror	ferebar	ferar	latus sum	latus eram
	ferris	ferebaris	fereris	latus es	latus eras
	fertur	ferebatur	feretur	latus est	latus erat
	ferimur	ferebamur	feremur	lati sumus	lati eramus
	ferimini	ferebamini	feremini	lati estis	lati eratis
	feruntur	ferebantur	ferentur	lati sunt	lati erant

Uses of verb + complement - note the use of the nominative

ille senex nobilis esse videtur.
That old man seems to be noble.

Augustus per multos annos princeps mansit.
Augustus remained *princeps f*or many years.

ille miles dux mox legetur.
That soldier will soon be chosen as general.

dux mortuus fertur.
The general is reported dead.

ille poeta sapiens vocatur.
That poet is called wise.

Exercise 7.1   Translate into English

1. ventus in urbem tempestatem fert.
2. discipuli libros magistro ferebant.
3. servi praemia regi ferent.
4. coniunx dona uxori tulit.
5. dux omnia arma iam tulerat.

Exercise 7.1E   Translate into English

1. venti in oppidum tempestates ferunt.
2. discipulus tres libros magistro ferebat.
3. filius praemium regi feret.
4. pueri pater multa dona magistro tulit.
5. princeps omnes gladios iam tulerat.

Exercise 7.2   Put the sentences in Ex 7.1 into the passive without translating

Exercise 7.2E   Put the sentences in Ex 7.1E into the passive without translating

1 ancilla quae in illa villa laborat per viam currit.
2 reginam quae irata semper est specto.
3 femina cuius pater agricola est vinum fert.
4 ancilla quacum saepe in oppidum eo tristissima est.
5 mulier cui heri donum pulchrum dedi miserrima est.

1 viri quorum dominus saevus est diu laborabant.
2. pueri quibuscum heri pugnavi in agro dormiunt.
3 hi sunt viri quos dominus saepe laudat.
4 hi sunt principes qui Romanos numquam laudant.
5 hi sunt senes quorum uxores saepe male se gerunt.

totus, tota, totum = whole, whole of
is declined like **unus** and **solus**

singular	masculine	feminine	neuter
nom.	totus	tota	totum
acc.	totum	totam	totum
gen.	totius	totius	totius
dat.	toti	toti	toti
abl.	toto	tota	toto
plural			
nom.	toti	totae	tota
acc.	totos	totas	tota
gen.	totorum	totarum	totorum
dat.	totis	totis	totis
abl.	totis	totis	totis

urbs tota deleta est.   The whole (of the) city was destroyed.

librum totum legi.   I have read the whole (of the) book.

Relative clauses and relative pronouns

Relative clauses in English are introduced by a relative pronoun (who, which) and refer back to a person or thing just mentioned, the antecedent.

There are two kinds of relative clause in English:

1. non restrictive

The teacher punished the boys, who had been naughty.

with a comma - the meaning is that the teacher punished all the boys mentioned.

2. restrictive

The teacher punished the boys who had been naughty.

without a comma - the meaning is the teacher punished only the naughty boys, and not the others.

Latin does not make this distinction

magister pueros qui mali fuerant punivit.

1 hic sunt feminae quibuscum saepe Romam eo.
2 uxores quas in oppido saepe video pulcherrimae sunt.
3 puellae quibus omnibus dona heri dedi pulchre cantant.
4 omnes ancillae quibuscum servi ludebant clamabant.
5 tres puellae quae a magistro punitae sunt iam flent.

Classical Latin did not have the level of punctuation we have today.

The relative pronoun in Latin must agree with its antecedent in its gender and number, but not necessarily in its case.

Compare

miles qui bene laborat validus est.   The soldier, who works well, is strong.

where **qui** is masc. sing. subject of **laborat** with

miles quem vides validus est.   The soldier (whom) you see is strong.

where **quem** is masc. sing. object of **vides**, so is in the accusative.

Note: quocum, quacum, quocum = with whom, with which
        quibuscum = with whom, with which

singular	masculine	feminine	neuter
nom.	qui	quae	quod
acc.	quem	quam	quod
gen.	cuius	cuius	cuius
dat.	cui	cui	cui
abl.	quo	qua	quo
plural			
nom.	qui	quae	quae
acc.	quos	quas	quae
gen.	quorum	quarum	quorum
dat.	quibus	quibus	quibus
abl.	quibus	quibus	quibus

The following sentences will provide examples of the relative pronouns in their different cases.

Exercise 7.3   Translate the following into English

1. vir qui fessus erat laborare nolebat.
2. paene tota urbs in bello deleta est.
3. locus totus in quo pueri ludunt pulcherrimus est.
4. haec pars oppidi quam omnes cives amant pulcherrima est.
5. ego illi mulieri cuius filia pulcherrima est multa dona dedi.
6. illum puerum quem punivit magister in oppido cum amicis saepe vidi.
7. fer, o serve, hos libros magistro qui in oppidum nunc est.
8. vidistine iuvenem quocum heri pugnavi?
9. hostes quibuscum pugnaverunt Romani celeriter effugerunt.
10. hae sunt puellae quibuscum saepe ludebam.

Exercise 7.3E   Translate the following into English

1. copiae quae fessae erant pugnare nolebant.
2. illi libri quos scripsit poeta notissimus pulcherrimi sunt.
3. locus in quo puellae ludebant pulcherrimus erat.
4. hoc est oppidum quod pauci cives amant.
5. ego viro cuius filiae pulcherrimae sunt multa dona dabam.
6. pueros quos punivit magister in media urbe conspexi.
7. ferte, o pueri, hos libros magistro qui in villa dormit.
8. vidistisne, o comites, iuvenes quibuscum heri pugnavi?
9. iuvenes quibuscum pugnaverunt milites fugerunt.
10. haec sunt arma quibus saepe pugnabam.

Exercise 7.4 Translate the following into Latin

1. The farmer was looking for the animals which had been in the field.
2. The slaves whom the master never praised ran away.
3. The walls that you can see were built by my slaves.
4. The city in which we used to live has been destroyed by the enemy.
5. The farmers who were working in this field had fought against the Romans.
6. My friend, give me the food that you have brought from the town.
7. I have brought all the gold that I found in the field.
8. All the citizens praised the general whose courage was well-known.
9. The man with whom I went to the town is my companion.
10. The farmer for whom I had brought the food was away.

Exercise 7.4E Translate the following into Latin

1. The maid-servants were looking for the animals that had escaped.
2. The boys whom the teacher often praised were happy.
3. That wall that I built yesterday has been destroyed by the storm.
4. The villa in which the queen used to live was destroyed in the war.
5. The slaves who were sleeping in the field had drunk a lot of wine.
6. Companions, give me the swords that you brought from the king.
7. My son, have you seen the spears that I found in the field?
8. The general who had been sent to Africa destroyed the whole city.
9. The woman with whom I went to the town is my sister.
10. The sailors for whom I brought the wine had already left.

is qui and ei qui

is qui = the one who, the man who, he who

Similarly

ea quae = she who, the woman who ; id quod = that which

eos qui bene laborant laudamus.
We praise those who work well.

Exercise 7.5 Translate the following into English

1. eos qui regem laudant non amamus.
2. nolite credere eis qui haec dicunt!
3. id quod difficile est saepe praemia fert.
4. illi iuvenes eas quae pulcherrimae sunt semper spectant.
5. nos eos qui celeriter currebant capere non poteramus.

1 hae sunt puellae quarum matres male se gesserunt.
2 hae sunt feminae tristes quae a coniugibus numquam laudantur.
3 haene sunt puellae quas Romae heri conspexisti?
4 noli laudare eas puellas quae male se gerunt.
5 hae sunt mulieres quorum coniuges semper absunt.

Chapter 8 idem, celer, alius, ipse, dum, note on the infinitive

idem = the same

is ea id with **-dem** added, with a change in the genitive plural

	masc.	fem.	neut.
singular			
nom.	idem	eadem	idem
acc.	eundem	eandem	idem
gen.	eiusdem	eiusdem	eiusdem
dat.	eidem	eidem	eidem
abl.	eodem	eadem	eodem
plural			
nom.	eidem	eaedem	eadem
acc.	eosdem	easdem	eadem
gen.	eorundem	earundem	eorundem
dat.	eisdem	eisdem	eisdem
abl.	eisdem	eisdem	eisdem

Examples:

regina idem iter semper facit.	The queen always makes the same journey.
eosdem agricolas in oppido vidi.	I saw the same farmers in the town.

Third declension adjectives ending in celer = quick, swift

	masc.	fem.	neut.
sing.			
nom.	celer	celeris	celere
voc.	celer	celeris	celere
acc.	celerem	celerem	celere
gen.	celeris	celeris	celeris
dat.	celeri	celeri	celeri
abl.	celeri	celeri	celeri
plural			
nom.	celeres	celeres	celeria
voc.	celeres	celeres	celeria
acc.	celeres	celeres	celeria
gen.	celerum	celerum	celerum
dat.	celeribus	celeribus	celeribus
abl.	celeribus	celeribus	celeribus

alius alia aliud = other

Like unus = one, solus = alone and totus = whole, alius needs careful attention

	masc.	fem.	neut.
singular			
nom.	alius	alia	aliud
acc.	alium	aliam	aliud
gen.	alius	alius	alius
dat.	alii	alii	alii
abl.	alio	alia	alio
plural			
nom.	alii	aliae	alia
acc.	alios	alias	alia
gen.	aliorum	aliarum	aliorum
dat.	aliis	aliis	aliis
abl.	aliis	aliis	aliis

Note:

In place of alius in the gen. sing. **alterius** is often used

1 magister dum pueri aderant dormiebat.
2 discipuli dum magister librum scribit discesserunt.
3 pueri dum magister librum legebat dormiverunt.
4 magister dum discipuli scribunt discessit.
5 pueri dum magister aderat dormiebant.

Examples:

hunc librum iam legi; fer mihi alium! I have already
read this book; bring me another (one).
alii milites fortiores his sunt. The other soldiers
are braver than these.

Note: alii ….. alii   some (men) …others

alii in via ambulabant, alii in villa dormiebant.
Some men were walking in the road, others
were sleeping in the villa.

Note also

alii cum aliis pugnant.
Some men are fighting some men and others
are fighting others.

1 vir dum in flumine stat pecuniam accepit.
2 senex cui femina pecuniam dederat valde iratus erat.
3 dum vir miser in via stat puella ei pecuniam dedit.
4 femina dum per viam ambulat pecuniam seni misero dedit.
5 regina dum per viam currit senem miserum vidit.

ipse ipsa ipsum = (-self)

ipse is used to emphasise the noun or pronoun

	masc.	fem.	neut.
singular			
nom.	ipse	ipsa	ipsum
acc.	ipsum	ipsam	ipsum
gen.	ipsius	ipsius	ipsius
dat.	ipsi	ipsi	ipsi
abl.	ipso	ipsa	ipso
plural			
nom.	ipsi	ipsae	ipsa
acc.	ipsos	ipsas	ipsa
gen.	ipsorum	ipsarum	ipsorum
dat.	ipsis	ipsis	ipsis
abl.	ipsis	ipsis	ipsis

1 dominus dum per viam ambulat uxorem conspexit.
2 servus dum ad oppidum festinat matrem conspexit.
3 pater dum Roma redit filium vidit.
4 dominus dum domum redit servum conspexit.
5 rex dum in proelio pugnat patrem subito conspexit.

Examples

ego ipse ducem vidi.	I myself saw the general.
regem ipsum in oppido conspexi.	I caught sight of the king himself in the town.
ipsae venient.	They themselves will come.

dum = while

There are two uses:

1. servi, dum dominus in villa dormiebat, in agro laborabant.
   While the master was sleeping in the villa, the slaves were working in the field.

Here while something was happening, something else was happening throughout the same period of time.

2. dum in via ambulo, clamorem magnum subito audivi.
   While I was walking in the street, I suddenly heard a great shout.

Note the present tense.

Here while something was happening, something new happened.

A note on the Infinitive

The present infinitive can often be translated by '...ing'
laborare in illis agris difficile est.
It is difficult to work in those fields.
Working in those fields is difficult.

celeriter currere seni difficile erat.
Running quickly was difficult for the old man.

Exercise 8.1 Translate into English

1. dum in urbem contendo, alios milites conspexi.
2. servi, dum dominus in villa laborat, omnes equos celeres ceperunt.
3. interea dux alias copias in monte reliquit.
4. rex ipse cenam uxori tulit.
5. ancillae, dum servi dormiebant, cenam parabant.
6. aliae ridebant, aliae dormiebant.
7. ego ipse eadem animalia in agrum heri pepuli.
8. paene omnes servi, dum custodes ludunt, effugerunt.
9. dum amicus me iuvat, aliud animal effugit.
10. alii milites intefecti sunt, alii vulnera saeva acceperunt.

1 puella dum mater et frater dormiebant legebat.
2 puer et puella dum mater aderat dormiebant.
3 puer dum soror dormiebat librum legebat.
4 mater dum filia dormiebat librum scribebat.
5 mater dum puer et puellae dormiunt discessit.

Exercise 8.1E Translate into English

1. interea, dum dux in oppidum contendit, alii milites discesserunt.
2. paene omnes servi, dum dominus in villa laborat, celeriter fugerunt.
3. dux alios milites prope flumen reliquit.
4. rex ipse nec vinum bibit nec cibum consumpsit.
5. regina, dum servi animalia in agrum pellunt, ex villa subito exit.
6. alii consumebant, alii bibebant.
7. ego regem ipsum in via heri vidi.
8. hae res eodem die gestae sunt.
9. tempestas eādem horā saepe advenit.
10. iuvenes celeres paene omnia animalia capere potuerunt.

Exercise 8.2 Translate into Latin

1. I caught sight of the same young man in the centre of the city.
2. Some boys were fighting, others were playing.
3. While I was reading a book, my friend arrived.
4. While the king was sleeping, the queen was reading a book.
5. I was unable to catch the swift boys.
6. We always see the same boys in the town.
7. The queen herself came to the town with her daughters.
8. I left the other books near the river.
9. Working in this bad light is very difficult.
10. Sailing to Italy will be easy.

29

Chapter 9 Past participle passive

In Chapter 5 we met the perfect passive tense, formed of the past participle passive PPP plus the present tense of sum. We can use the **past participle passive** on its own – with the meaning of **having been ....**

Thus: **amatus** = having been loved   **monitus** = having been warned
The PPP is an adjective and must agree with the subject. Its endings are the same as those of **bonus**

Thus:

1 coniunx reginae in urbe conspectus iam domum redibat.
2 servus in urbe a domino conspectus quam celerrime fugit.
3 rex ab uxore in urbe conspectus iam ad villam currebat.
4 nauta ab aquila vulneratus iam miserrimus fuit.
5 agricola a domino punitus iam miser fuit.

urbs **capta** deleta est. = Literally: The city **having been captured** was destroyed.

This translation sounds a little unnatural. We can say

When the city had been captured, it was destroyed *or*
The city which had been captured was destroyed *or*
The city was captured and destroyed.

Depending upon the context, the PPP can have the meaning of

when *the city had been destroyed ....*   temporal
because *the city had been destroyed ....*   causal
although *the city had been destroyed ....*   concessive

Compare

pueri saevissime puniti magistrum amabant.
Although the boys had been very savagely punished they loved the teacher.

with

pueri saevissime puniti magistrum non amabant.
Because the boys had been very savagely punished, they did not love their teacher.

Exercise 9.1 Translate into English

1. servi felices, a domino nobili liberati, laeti erant.
2. miles, dux a comitibus factus, superbe se gessit.
3. senes ab omnibus comitibus relicti quam celerrime effugerunt.
4. rex superbus de periculo a comitibus monitus se bene gerere constituit.
5. hunc murum a servis aedificatum cras delebo.
6. milites ab hostibus vulnerati muros custodiebant.
7. dux milites in proelio interfectos magnopere laudavit.

8. servi miseri, a domino laborare iussi, statim fugerunt.

9. paene omnes cives, ab hostibus vulnerati, ex urbe fugerunt.

10. oppidum diu oppugnatum tandem captum est.

Exercise 9.1E Translate into English

1. ventus navem tempestate deletam ad insulam pepulit.
2. agricola omnia animalia in agro relicta diu petivit.
3. princeps omnia arma ad oppidum lata statim cepit.
4. regina superba a filia monita statim fugit.
5. haec templa duobus mensibus aedificata
   tempestate celeriter deleta sunt.
6. hostes muros fortiter a civibus custoditos deleverunt.
7. somnus milites in proelio victos tandem cepit.
8. equus ingens prope muros relictus in urbem ductus est.
9. naves nec ventis nec tempestatibus deletae
   tandem ad Britanniam advenerunt.
10. alios libros a magistro laudatos tribus diebus legi.

1 senis a rege laborare iussus villam aedificabat.
2 ancilla a domino conspecta ad villam festinavit.
3 princeps a servo de muro monitus perterritus erat.
4 servus a domino laborare iussus murum parvum aedificabat.
5 servus a principe stare iussus murum custodiebat.

Exercise 9.2 Translate into Latin

1. After the ship had been driven to the island it was destroyed by the inhabitants.
2. After the city had been attacked for two months it was finally destroyed by the enemy.
3. After the general had been warned about the danger, he departed immediately.
4. I shall give prizes to the boys who have been praised by the teacher.
5. The swift horses which had been captured yesterday were led to the town.
6. We saw the slaves who had been set free by their master.
7. We looked at a part of the city that had been destroyed by the enemy.
8. Within three days I shall read the books brought to me by my friend.
9. My son, bring me the weapons that have been prepared by the slaves!
10. Where is the money that has been given by the queen?

1 regina ab coniuge ad oppidum ire iussa vinum iam ferebat.
2 ancilla a rege punita laborare nolebat.
3 ancilla ab domino vinum ferre iussa iam celeriter redibat.
4 ancilla a coniuge relicta miserrima erat.
5 puella ab aquila vulnerata domum celeriter currebat.

1 equus pro muro relictus iam dormiebat.
2 cur equum in agro relictum cepisti?
3 equus in via relictus ab aquila interfectus est.
4 equum in via relictum heri vidi.
5 equa in via relicta aquilam subito conspexit.

Chapter 10   Present participle active

Latin has a **present participle active** (e.g. warning) and a **past participle passive** (e.g. having been warned). The present particle passive (e.g. being warned) and the past participle active (e.g. having warned) do not exist in Latin. Here we shall meet the present participle active.

Note that English verbal form ending in '-ing' has two completely different meanings:

As a participle: The girls were walking to the sea, *laughing*.

As a verbal noun   *Singing* is good for you.

Latin does not use a participle in this second case.

1 heri ancillam in via stantem conspexi.
2 hodie puellam aquam domum ferentem conspeximus.
3 subito filiam magistri vinum ferentem vidimus.
4 puellam pulchram in via dormientem conspeximus.
5 mulieri per viam festinanti donum non dedi.

The present participle of amo **amans** is declined like **ingens**

	masc.	fem.	neut.
Singular			
nom.	amans	amans	amans
voc.	amans	amans	amans
acc.	amantem	amantem	amans
gen.	amantis	amantis	amantis
dat.	amanti	amanti	amanti
abl.	amanti	amanti	amanti
Plural			
nom.	amantes	amantes	amantia
voc.	amantes	amantes	amantia
acc.	amantes	amantes	amantia
gen.	amantium	amantium	amantium
dat.	amantibus	amantibus	amantibus
abl.	amantibus	amantibus	amantibus

To form the present participle take off **-re** from the infinitive and add **-ns**. Hence:

amans, monens, regens, audiens, capiens

Note: **iens** participle from **eo** (I go) declined:
iens euntem euntis eunti eunti
euntes euntes euntium euntibus euntibus
Note compounds: exiens, iniens, rediens, transiens

Examples:

1 mulier militi in via stani pecuniam dedit.
2 mulier pecuniam viro in via stanti dare noluit.
3 vir miser in via stans pecuniam accepit.
4 puella senem in muro sedentem de periculo monuit.
5 regina senem pecuniam capientem non laudavit.

dux in proelio **pugnans** interfectus est.
The leader was killed *fighting*   in the battle.
                whilst fighting / as he was fighting

ducem ad urbem **redeuntem** conspeximus.
We caught sight of the general *(as he was)*
returning to the city.

turbam iuvenum ex oppido **fugientium** vidimus.
We saw a crowd of young men fleeing the town.

Exercise 10.1 Translate into English

1. paene omnes milites ab oppido discedentes
   princeps conspexit.
2. puer praemia spectans ridebat.
3. viri pessimi pecuniam nostram capientes ridebant.
4. cives principem bene se gerentem amabant.
5. pueri in villa dormientes tuti erant.
6. dux milites totam noctem templum custodientes laudavit.
7. nautae clamantes ad navem lati sunt.
8. milites fortiter pugnantes in proelio saevo intefecti sunt.
9. mater filios in via ludentes conspexit.
10. dux milites effugientes redire coegit.

1 puellae per viam ambulantes ridebant.
2 filios reginae in oppidum ineuntes vidimus.
3 ancillas in agros fugientes cepimus
4 puellas miseras in via pereuntes vidimus.
5 hodie duas puellas per viam currentes conspeximus.

1 senex crudelis puellas dormientes saeve punire constituit.
2 pueri magistrum ridentem spectaverunt.
3 puer magistrum stantem spectavit.
4 magister iratus pueros dormientes spectavit.
5 dominus puerum et puellam dormientes conspexit.

Exercise 10.1E   Translate into English

1. omnes gentes in oppidum ruentes custos conspexit.
2. pueri tempestatem saevam spectantes perterriti erant.
3. iuvenes mali omne aurum capientes ridebant.
4. cives regem male se gerentem ex urbe pepulerunt.
5. puellae in villa dormientes tutae non erant.
6. rex custodes totam noctem in muro manentes laudavit.
7. gentes fortiter clamantes ad regem latae sunt.
8. omnes duces fortiter pugnantes tandem interfecti sunt.
9. frater sororem in via ludentem conspexit.
10. pater filium dormientem vidit.

Exercise 10.1E   Translate into Latin

1. We caught sight of the slaves as they rushed along the street.
2. The young men heard the shouts of the soldiers as they stood in the street.
3. The slave killed the brave general as he slept.
4. The enemy attacked the sailors as they sailed to Italy.
5. The proud mother watched her sons playing in the field.
6. The animals frightened the maids as they walked down the road.
7. The young men threw spears at the guards who were sleeping near the wall.
8. The guards saw the soldiers as they crossed the river.
9. The general praised his soldiers as they captured the animals.
10. We saw the boys going into the country-house.

Chapter 11   The imperfect subjunctive and purpose clauses

In Latin we have learned that there are two **voices** – **active** (he sees) and **passive** (he is seen). There are also three **moods**. We have already met two: the **indicative** and the **imperative**.

The **indicative mood** is used to express a fact:

princeps multos annos rexit.
The chieftain ruled for many years.

The **imperative mood** issues a command:

fer mihi vinum!
Bring me wine!

1 puellae tristes domum redierunt ut fratrem viderent.
2 filiae miserae regis ad agrum fugerunt ne a patre punirentur.
3 feminae ad villam cucurrerunt ut e senibus malis effugerent.
4 pueri currebant ut ante noctemad villem advenirent.
5 puellae quam celerrime currebant ut equos viderent.

The third mood is called the **subjunctive** and is used to express a purpose, a fear, a wish, a request – something that might happen.

There is a corresponding subjunctive mood for most tenses of the indicative. For the moment we shall concentrate on the **imperfect subjunctive**.

ACTIVE					
amarem	monerem	regerem	audirem	caperem	essem
amares	moneres	regeres	audires	caperes	esses
amaret	moneret	regeret	audiret	caperet	esset
amaremus	moneremus	regeremus	audiremus	caperemus	essemus
amaretis	moneretis	regeretis	audiretis	caperetis	essetis
amarent	monerent	regerent	audirent	caperent	essent

PASSIVE					
amarer	monerer	regerer	audirer	caperer	
amareris	monereris	regereris	audireris	capereris	
amaretur	moneretur	regeretur	audiretur	caperetur	
amaremur	moneremur	regeremur	audiremur	caperemur	
amaremini	moneremini	regeremini	audiremini	caperemini	
amarentur	monerentur	regerentur	audirentur	caperentur	

In Latin **purpose clauses** which are in the past, the main clause is as normal in the indicative, but the verb in the purpose clause goes into the **imperfect subjunctive**.

Example

Main clause	purpose clause
venimus	**ut** regem videremus.
We came	**in order to** see the king.
milites venerunt	**ut** pugnarent.
The soldiers came	**to** fight.
servus fugit	**ne** laboraret.
The slave fled	**in order not to** work.

1 pater et filius hasta iaciebant ut phocam interficerent.
2 agricolae tela tenebant ut animalia occiderent.
3 pueri mali sagittas iecerunt ut aquilas necarent.
4 viri hastas iaciebant ut animalia vulnerarent.
5 nautae tela iaciebant ne a phoca vinceretur.

Note the negative **ne** = **in order not**

In English we can translate **ut** by *to, in order to, so as to* and **ne** *in order not to, so as not to, to stop being, so that (they) would not be*

Exercise 11.1   Translate into English

1. cives ad mediam urbem contenderunt ut reginam viderent.
2. Romani fortiter pugnaverunt ut hostes vincerent.
3. servi celeriter effugerunt ne a domino punirentur.
4. iuvenes in agrum animalia pepulerunt ut ea ibi necarent.
5. milites in oppido convenerunt ut alium ducem legerent.
6. milites statim fugerunt ne ab hostibus caperentur.
7. cives ex urbe quam celerrime exierunt ut hostes effugerent.
8. gens murum ingentem ut urbem defenderet aedificavit.
9. puer ad oppidum cum patre iit ne in villa solus esset.
10. omnia arma in urbem lata sunt ut cives se defenderent.

1 uxor fugit ne coniunx eam peteret.
2 dux militum clamabat ut puella pecuniam traderet.
3 nauta saevus puellam terrebat ut pecuniam traderet.
4 puella perterrita fugit ne pecuniam traderet.
5 femina agricolae saevo pecuniam dedit ne ab eo puniretur

Exercise 11.1E   Translate into English

1. rex ad medium oppidum contendit ut comitem videret.
2. cives celeriter convenerunt ut servos novos conspicerent.
3. hostes celeriter effugerunt ne a nobis vincerentur.
4. agricolae alia animalia ex oppido pepulerunt ne cives perterriti essent.
5. milites eidem in oppidum contenderunt ut ducem iterum viderent.
6. custodes statim fugerunt ne ab hostibus interficerentur.
7. paene omnes cives ex urbe discesserunt ut hostes effugerent.
8. milites ut valida corpora haberent multum cibi boni consumebant.
9. puella in villa mansit ut sola esset.
10. omnes hastae et sagittae ad villam latae sunt ut dux se defenderet.

Exercise 11.2   **Translate into Latin**

1. We went to town to see the prizes.
2. Almost all the citizens ran away in order not to be captured by the enemy.
3. The soldiers brought the slaves back to the town in order to punish them.
4. The wretched slaves ran away so as not to be killed by their master.
5. We handed over the books in order not to be punished by the teacher.
6. The allies returned to the city so as to see the general.
7. The poet remained in his country-house to write a new book.
8. The general took all the weapons in order to defend himself well.
9. The general collected his troops in front of the walls in order to attack the city.
10. We worked for two hours in order to make a gift for the teacher.

A note on purpose clauses

In translating a sentence such as 'He sent slaves to work in the fields', instead of saying:

servos misit ut in agris laborarent

it is more common to say

servos misit **qui** in agris laborarent

1 ancilla aquam ferebat ut equus biberet.
2 puella vinum portabat ut rex biberet.
3 poeta vinum ferebat ne rex iratus esset.
4 filia principis vinum ferebat ut aquila biberet.
5 frater regis equo tulit ut phoca biberet.

If there is a comparative in the purpose clause, **quo** must be used rather than ut:

dux his militibus, quo melius pugnarent, tela optima dedit.
The general gave the best weapons to these soldiers in order that they could fight better.

Exercise 11.3   **Translate into English**

1. pater Romam filium qui cum fratre ibi laboraret misit.
2. dux ad urbem milites optimos qui eam fortiter defenderent contendere iussit.
3. magister libros optimos discipulis quo melius scriberent ostendit.
4. dominus servum quo celerius curreret laudavit.
5. dux haec verba militibus quo audacius pugnarent dixit.
6. rex ipse ad urbem quo milites fortius muros defenderent advenit.
7. rex ad agros milites quo agricolae tutius laborarent misit.
8. dux ad oppidum milites qui muros delerent misit.
9. pater filium quo melius laboraret saevissime punivit.
10. dux optima tela militibus quo rem facilius gererent tradidit.

Exercise 11.4   **Translate into Latin**

1. The general sent a messenger to tell the king about the danger.
2. The king himself praised his soldiers in order that they fight better.
3. The leader sent soldiers to overcome the enemy.
4. The guards were standing on the walls in order to see the enemy more easily.

Chapter 12   Indirect commands

So far we have met only direct commands or imperatives:

serve, fer mihi illos libros!   Bring me those books!

We can make this an indirect command by

I asked the slave to bring me those books.

We could write:

servum illos libros mihi ferre iussi.
I ordered the slave to bring me those books.

or

1 nauta iratus reginam ut discederet rogavit.
2 agricola audax reginae ut maneret persuasit.
3 femina senem laetum ut sederet persuasit.
4 dux ancillae ut cantaret imperavit.
5 femina nautae ut ibi maneret persuasit.

servum illos libros mihi ferre coegi.
I forced the slave to bring me those books.

We can also use such verbs as **rogavi** (I asked), **monui** (I advised) and two new verbs:

> impero -are -avi -atum *(+dat.)* = I command, I order
> persuadeo -ere persuasi persuasum *(+dat.)* = I persuade

with **ut** and the **subjunctive**; negative **ne**

dux militibus ut oppidum statim oppugnarent imperavit.
The general ordered the soldiers to attack the town immediately.

magister pueros ne iterum clamarent monuit.
The teacher warned the boys not to shout again.

Exercise 12.1   Translate into English

1. magister sapiens discipulos ut libros optimos legerent monuit.
2. iuvenes eosdem ut ab media urbe discesserent meus pater rogavit.
3. num cives vobis ut animalia in flumen iacerent imperaverunt?
4. princeps ipse omnibus militibus ut in urbe manerent persuasit.
5. nonne dux vobis ut urbem defenderetis rogavit?
6. cur princeps tibi ut flumen transires imperavit?
7. quis tibi ut animalia in agrum pelleres imperavit?
8. dux militibus audacibus ut in hostes tertia hora ruerent imperavit.
9. magister discipulis ut se bene gererent persuasit.

10. rex iratus servis ut cibum pararent imperavit.

Exercise 12.1E   Translate into English

1. pater filium ne libros pessimos legeret monuit.
2. custos milites eosdem ut ab medio oppido discesserent rogavit.
3. num dux vobis ut oppidum oppugnaretis imperavit?
4. regina ipsa filio ut maneret in urbe persuasit.
5. nonne rex vobis ut in urbe maneretis rogavit?
6. cur custos tibi ut in flumen te iaceres imperavit?
7. quis tibi ut animalibus cibum ferres imperavit?
8. dominus servis ut cibum equis pararent imperavit.
9. magister pueris ut bene scriberent persuasit.
10. rex servum ut arma pararet rogavit.

Exercise 12.2   Translate into Latin

1. We advised the boys to read these books.
2. The king ordered the slaves to take all the gold.
3. Who ordered your troops to leave the city?
4. We persuaded the teacher not to punish the pupils.
5. The king asked the slaves to prepare the weapons.
6. Surely the general didn't order you to attack the city?
7. The parents persuaded their sons to behave themselves.
8. The mother told the girls not to play in the street.
9. I advised the king not to leave the city.
10. Surely you told the pupils to work well?

1 agricola ancillae pulchrae ut discederet persuasit.
2 agricola feminae pulchrae ut ibi maneret persuasit.
3 nauta mulieri nobili ut maneret in oppido imperavit.
4 senex mulieri iratae ut statim abiret rogavit.
5 agricola puellam ne fugeret monuit.

1 dominus viris ut dormirent persuaserat.
2 magister discipulos laborare iusserat.
3 dominus servis ut murum aedificarent imperaverat.
4 magister pueros fessos ne dormirent monuerat.
5 princeps filiis ut murum aedificarent imperaverat.

1 regina ancillae ut murum deleret imperaverat.
2 dominus servo ut villam quam celerrime aedificaret persuaserat.
3 pater filium miserum ut villam aedificaret rogaverat.
4 dominus servo ut murum aedificaret imperaverat.
5 servus regem ut oppidum novum aedificaret rogaverat.

Chapter 13   Ablative absolute

The **ablative absolute** construction consists of a **past participle passive (PPP)** or a **present participle active** agreeing with a **noun** in the ablative. It is important to note that these words must not be related to any other words in the sentence.

urbe deleta Romani discesserunt.
The city having been destroyed, the Romans departed.

Of course, a more natural translation would be:

With the city destroyed …. or When the city had been destroyed ….. or Once the city had been destroyed …..

filio ludente mater librum legit.
The mother read a book while her son was playing.

Note that in the ablative absolute construction, the present participle ends in **-e** rather than **-i**

Note that there is no present participle of sum. It can be simply *understood.* In the sentence

When Caesar was leader, the soldiers were very happy.
We can translate it as: Caesar (being) leader …..

Caesare duce, milites laetissimi erant.

Exercise 13.1 Translate these phrases using 'when … had been …'

1. praemiis acceptis …
2. clamoribus auditis ….
3. armis captis ….
4. copiis collectis ….
5. hostibus conspectis….
6. die constituto ….
7. cibo consumpto ….
8. urbe defensa ….
9. oppido deleto ….
10. verbis dictis ….
11. equis ductis
12. itinere facto
13. bello gesto ….
14. hastis iactis ….
15. auro invento ….
16. milite iusso ….
17. libro lecto ….
18. nuntio misso ….
19. gladiis motis ….
20. militibus occisis
21. auro ostento
22. libris positis ….
23. militibus reductis ….
24. urbe recta ….
25. libro scripto ….
26. servis traditis ….
27. monte viso ….
28. animali coacto ….
29. iuvene custodito ….
30. principe interfecto ….
31. navibus pulsis ….
32. puella petita ….
33. auro relicto ….
34. urbe oppugnata ….

Exercise 13.2 Translate these phrases using 'While ….. was …..'

1. pueris praemia accipientibus ….

2. duce domum adveniente ….

3. principe appropinquante ….

4. animalibus clamores audientientis ….

5. milite arma capiente ….

6. duce milites colligente ….

7. nautis insulam conspicientibus ….

8. duce hoc constituente ….

9. custode ad urbem contendente ….

10. civibus in oppido convenientibus ….

11. equo celeriter currente ….

12. militibus muros custodientibus ….

13. civibus urbem defendentibus ….

14. hostibus oppidum delentibus ….

15. patre hoc dicente ….

16. gente ex oppido discedente ….

17. Tarqinio rege ….

18. animalibus agrum effugientibus ….

19. matre exeunte ….

20. amico me exspectante ….

21. nauta hanc rem faciente ….

22. iuvenibus ad oppidum festinantibus ….

23. hostibus fugientibus ….

24. duce has res male gerente ….

25. custode ducem interficiente ….

26. agricola aurum inveniente ….

27. deo iuvante ….

28. patre in oppido laborante ….

29. magistro hoc iubente ….

30. poeta hunc librum legente ….

31. domino servum liberante ….

32. pueris in via ludentibus ….

33. matre in villa manente ….

34. rege nuntium mittente ….

35. servo regem monente ….

36. nautis navigantibus ….

37. magistro hoc narrante ….

38. agricola animal necante ….

39. custode haec nuntiante ….

40. hostibus cives occidentibus ….

41. hostibus oppidum oppugnantibus ….

42. fratre librum ostendente ….

43. ancilla cibum parante ….

44. tempestate navem pellente ….

45. animali in agro pereunte ….

46. servo dominum petente ….

47. militibus in oppido pugnantibus ….

48. magistro discipulos puniente ….

49. principe Romam redeunte ….

50. agricola animalia reducente ….

51. principe Romae regente ….

52. puero praemium relinquente ….

53. puella respondente ….

54. discipulis ridentibus ….

55. animali ad servum ruente ….

56. magistro me salutuante ….

57. puero scribente ….

58. patre filiam servante ….

59. nauta mare spectante ….

60. hostibus Romanos superantibus ….

61. animalibus pueros terrentibus ….

62. domino servos tradente ….

63. milite flumen transeunte ….

64. amico Romam veniente ….

65. sociis periculum videntibus ….

66. militibus hostes vincentibus ….

67. matre filium vocante ….

68. milite senem vulnerante ….

Chapter 14 Present infinitive passive

Corresponding to the present infinitive active (e.g. spectare = to watch), there is a present infinitive passive (e.g. to be watched)

	Present infinitive active		Present infinitive passive	
1	amare	to love	amari	to be loved
2	monere	to warn	moneri	to be warned
3	regere	to rule	regi	to be ruled
4	audire	to hear	audiri	to be heard
3½	capere	to take	capi	to be taken

Note that there is no present infinitive passive of facio

Exercise 14.1 Translate into English

1. dux a militibus audiri nolebat.
2. clamores audiri non possunt.
3. cives capi nolunt.
4. animalia cogi in agrum non poterant.
5. animalia colligi nolebant.
6. mulier conspici nolebat.
7. dux hunc cibum consumi iussit.
8. dux muros fortiter custodi iussit.
9. rex urbem defendi iusserat.
10. princeps oppidum deleri non iubebit.
11. animal per viam duci noluit.
12. dux bellum geri cum hostibus statim iussit.
13. hae hastae in oppidum iaci non possunt.
14. aurum inveniri non poterit.
15. dux servos interfici iussit.
16. magister omnes libros legi iussit.
17. rex nuntium mitti Romam iussit.
18. dominus servum occidi iubebit.
19. dux aurum regi ostendi nolebat.
20. animal in hoc loco poni noluit.
21. equus pelli a puero non vult.
22. rex aurum in illo loco peti iussit.
23. equi ad urbem reduci noluerunt.
24. Romani a regibus regi non iam volebant.
25. pueri Romae relinqui nolebant.
26. poeta hunc librum scribi non cupivit.

Exercise 14.2 Translate into Latin

1. The soldiers don't want to be captured by the enemy.
2. The chief ordered the soldiers to be collected near the wall.
3. The bad master ordered the slaves to be killed.
4. The king ordered the walls of the town to be destroyed.
5. These pupils do not want to be punished by the teacher.
6. The girls did not want to be left in Rome.
7. The king ordered the gold to be sent to the city.
8. The teacher ordered the books to be read by all the pupils.
9. The horses don't want to be driven by the boys.
10. The general saw that all the ships were being destroyed by the storm.

Chapter 15   Deponent verbs

A deponent verb is a verb which is passive in form but active in meaning. In nearly all its parts it has the appearance of being passive.

hortor -ari -atus sum = I encourage

present	imperfect	future	perfect	pluperfect
hortor	hortabar	hortabor	hortatus sum	hortatus eram
hortaris	hortabaris	hortaberis	hortatus es	hortatus eras
hortatur	hortabatur	hortabitur	hortatus est	hortatus erat
hortamur	hortabamur	hortabimur	hortati sumus	hortati eramus
hortamini	hortabamini	hortabimini	hortati estis	hortati eratis
hortantur	hortabantur	hortabuntur	hortati sunt	hortati erant

infinitive: hortari

other deponent verbs

conor, conari, conatus sum	1	I try
egredior, egredi, egressus sum	3½	I go out, leave
ingredior, ingredi, ingressus sum	3½	I go in, enter
loquor, loqui, locutus sum	3	I speak
morior, mori, mortuus sum	3½	I die
patior, pati, passus sum	3½	I suffer, endure
sequor, sequi, secutus sum	3	I follow
proficiscor, proficisci, profectus sum	3	I set out
progredior, progredi, progressus sum	3½	I go forward, advance

Exercise 15.1 Translate into English

1. matrem ut statim discederet hortabar.
2. dux tertia hora egressus est.
3. Romani in bellum duobus annis ingedientur.
4. senes duas horas locuti sunt.
5. novem milites in proelio mortui sunt.
6. clamores saevos animalium diu passi sumus.
7. senes tres horas secuti sumus.
8. milites duabus horis proficiscentur.
9. copiae hostium lente progrediebantur.
10. quattuor diebus proficisci conabor.

Exercise 15.1E Translate into English

1. pater filium ut statim laboraret hortatus est.
2. milites secunda hora egredienter.
3. agricola quartus in villam duabus horis ingedietur.
4. mulieres iratae duas horas locutae erant.
5. regina in villa subito mortua est.
6. parentes clamores saevos puellarum parvarum omnem diem passi sunt.
7. viros celeres tres horas secuti sumus.
8. dux duabus horis ad montes proficiscetur.
9. paene omnes copiae ad flumen progressae sunt.
10. rex tribus diebus in itinere longo proficisci conabitur.

Exercise 15.2 Translate into Latin

1. The general always used to encourage his soldiers to fight bravely.
2. Many men tried to catch the animals but in vain.
3. We'll set out from the city at first light.
4. The enemy entered the town in the middle of the night.
5. We tried to sail to the island in these ships.
6. The father encouraged his sons to work well.
7. I shall try to build the wall tomorrow.
8. The general ordered the troops to advance as quickly as possible.
9. The old man had suffered many harsh things.
10. The teacher spoke about the battle to his pupils.

Present and past participles of deponent verbs

I   The present participle

The **present participle** has the **active form**, hence conans = trying, loquens = speaking, sequens = following etc.

Latin present participles are often best translated by a clause. So

feminas in via loquentes audivimus.

We heard the women as they spoke in the street.

Exercise 15.3 Translate into English

1. ducem milites hortantem audivimus.
2. puer, iuva servum opus suum facere conantem!
3. milites ex oppido egredientes conspeximus.
4. mulieres in villa loquentes nos effugimus.

5. copiis ad montem proficiscientibus paene omnes cives dormiebant.
6. hostibus effugere conantibus dux Romanus oppidum oppugnare constituit.
7. nolite credere viris haec loquentibus!
8. hostes copias proficiscentes subito petiverunt.
9. filius patrem ingredientem salutavit.
10. custodes viros ad oppidum progredientes hastis pepulerunt.

2   The past participle

As we have mentioned before, Latin does not have a past participle active. So 'Having reached the city, the soldiers …..' would have to be translated as 'When they had reached the city, the soldiers …' Deponent verbs however, passive in form but active in meaning, do allow us to translate such sentences as

The enemy, having advanced for two hours, suddenly fled.

hostes duas horas progressi subito fugerunt.

Exercise 15.4 Translate into English

1. miles multa vulnera passus tandem mortuus est.
2. servus saepe effugere conatus sed frustra, manere constituit.
3. senes multas horas locuti tandem domum discesserunt.
4. milites in itinere longo profecti magnopere iam fessi erant.
5. copiae prima luce profectae tribus horis ad flumen advenerunt.
6. iuvenes viros trans montes secuti tandem eos prope flumen conspexerunt.
7. dominus puerum praemia capere conatum saeve punivit.
8. milites virum multa saeva passum reduxerunt.
9. milites nostri hostes oppidum oppugnare conantes petiverunt.
10. turba mulierum ab urbe prima luce profectarum quinque horas ambulavit.

Exercise 15.5 Translate into English

1. is reginam milites hortantem numquam audivit.
2. turba iuvenum ab oppido prima luce profectorum tres horas ambulavit.
3. pueri, iuvate senem opus suum facere conantem!
4. viri paene omnes milites oppidum oppugnare conantes interfecerunt.
5. gentes ex oppido egredientes dux conspexit.
6. magister pueros praemia delere conatos saevissime punivit.
7. ex iuvenibus in via loquentibus pueri effugerunt.
8. nautae iuvenes trans mare secuti tandem eos in insula conspexerunt.
9. militibus ad flumen proficiscentibus paene omnes cives in media urbe manserunt.
10. mulieres prima luce profectae paucis horis ad flumen advenerunt.
11. copiis hostium effugere conantibus dux Graecus urbem oppugnare constituit.
12. milites tribus antea horis progressi celeriter ad locum advenerunt.
13. noli credere puero haec verba loquenti!
14. coniuges multas horas locuti domum redierunt.

15. milites viros proficiscentes subito magnis telis petiverunt.
16. ancilla animal pellere conata sed frustra, ad villam rediit.
17. filia matrem in templum ingredientem salutavit.
18. milites multa et saeva vulnera passi tandem mortui sunt.
19. custos virum ad oppidum progredientem telis pepulit.
20. miles celer iuvenem sequens telo interfectus est.

Exercise 15.6 Translate into Latin

1. The guard was killed as he was setting out on his journey.
2. The husband greeted his wife as she entered the country-house.
3. Having set out at first light, the soldiers finally arrived at the sea.
4. Having advanced for two hours, the soldiers finally reached the city.
5. Having tried in vain to enter the city, the enemy went away in the middle of the night.
6. O king, don't believe the words of that evil general!
7. As the pupils were trying to run away, the teacher caught sight of them.
8. After following the animal for an hour, the boy finally threw a spear.
9. The enemy killed the soldiers as they were entering the harbour.
10. The enemy threw many arrows at the soldiers as they were advancing.

Chapter 16   Fourth declension nouns; indirect statements

Fourth declension nouns

There is only a small group of nouns in the fourth declension. We concentrate on

exercitus m.	= army
manus f.	= hand
portus m.	= harbour
domus f.	= house *(See Ch. 3 and box below)*

	singular	plural
nom.	portus	portus
voc.	portus	portus
acc.	portum	portus
gen.	portus	portuum
dat.	portui	portibus
abl.	portu	portibus

	singular	plural
nom.	domus	domus
voc.	domus	domus
acc.	domum	domus
gen.	domus *or* domi	domorum
dat.	domui *or* domo	domibus
abl.	domo	domibus

Indirect Statements: accusative and present infinitive

He says: 'Caesar is approaching.'

The actual words that are used by the speaker are in **direct speech**. Putting this into **indirect speech**:

He says that Caesar is approaching.

Latin puts the noun 'Caesar' into the accusative case and the verb 'is approaching' into the present infinitive; there is no verb for *that* here.

Thus:

Caesarem appropinquare dicit.

This construction is used not only after verbs of 'speaking' but also verbs like 'writing, thinking etc' followed by *that*. Such verbs as:

audio, clamo, credo, dico, invenio, lego, narro, nuntio, respondeo, scribo, video

plus two new verbs

scio scire scivi scitum 4   = I know
nescio nescire nescivi nescitum 4 = I do not know

Exercise 16.1   Translate into English

1. scio domum magistri parvam esse.
2. poeta scribit principem bene regere.
3. credisne regem in insula esse?
4. audio exercitum in urbe adesse.
5. omnes cives dicunt hostes appropinquare.
6. dux semper respondet milites has res nescire.
7. senex clamat milites discedere.
8. scisne exercitum hostium in portu adesse?
9. rex audit aurum non iam in villa esse.
10. plurimi dicunt reginae manus pulchras esse.

All the main verbs in the sentences of Ex 16.1 are in the present tense. The present infinitive indicates that this action is going on at the same time as the main verb in the sentence. This also applies when the main verb is not in the present tense. For example, in the sentence

I **knew** that the army **was** coming.

the 'knowing' and 'was coming' are happening at the same time, hence

sciebam exercitum venire.
I **knew** that the army **was** coming.

puer clamavit iuvenes discedere.
The boy **shouted** that the young men **were** leaving.

Exercise 16.2   Translate into English

1. quis sciebat virum domi esse?
2. poeta narravit principem bene regere.
3. credebasne Romam insulam esse?
4. audivi exercitum ad urbem progredi.
5. omnes cives dicebant hostes proficisci.
6. dux superbus semper respondebat milites suos has res nescire.

7. senex clamavit milites discedere.
8. sciebasne exercitum hostium ad portum progredi?
9. rex nuntiavit urbem iam in manibus hostium esse.
10. plurimi dixerunt regi manus minimas esse.

Exercise 16.3 Translate into Latin

1. The messenger says that the enemy are approaching.
2. O slave, do you know that the master is at home?
3. The leader knows that the ships are in the harbour.
4. The general announces that the enemy army is in front of the city wall.
5. The young men said that the old men were in the centre of the city.
6. All the pupils knew that their teacher was in Rome.
7. I didn't know that the boy had all the prizes.
8. Very many men said that the storm was fierce.
9. The king said that the guards were very brave.
10. The old man says that he drinks a lot of wine.

Chapter 17   Perfect infinitive, active and passive

Perfect infinitive active

		perfect	perfect infinitive active	English
1	amo	amavi	amavisse	to have loved
2	moneo	monui	monuisse	to have warned
3	rego	rexi	rexisse	to have ruled
4	audio	audivi	audivisse	to have heard
3½	capio	cepi	cepisse	to have taken
	sum	fui	fuisse	to have been

Perfect infinitive passive

		PPP	Perfect Infinitive Passive	English
1	amo	amatus	amatus esse	to have been loved
2	moneo	monitus	monitus esse	to have been warned
3	rego	rectus	rectus esse	to have been ruled
4	audio	auditus	auditus esse	to have been heard
3½	capio	captus	captus esse	to have been taken

Since the perfect passive participle is an adjectival form, it has to agree with the subject, which may be in the accusative in an indirect statement.

The **perfect infinitive** indicates that this action took place **before** that of the main verb. Thus,

scio puerum advenisse.
I **know** that the boy **has** arrived.

sciebat puerum advenisse.
I **knew** that the boy **had** arrived.

audivi hostes victos esse.
I **heard** that the enemy **had been** defeated.

pater mihi dixit reginam mortuam esse.
My father **told** me that the queen **had** died.

Note that since there is a perfect participle passive of facio **factus -a -um**, there is a perfect infinitive passive of facio: factus esse

scio haec ad puero malo facta esse.
I know that these things have been done by the naughty boy.

We can say that the perfect infinitive goes one step further back that the main verb.

Exercise 17.1 Translate into English

1. nuntius dicit hostes urbem cepisse.
2. frater nuntiavit portum ab hostibus captum esse.
3. paene omnes cives iam sciunt principem mortuum esse.
4. omnes discipuli nesciebant magistrum librum clarissimum scripsisse.
5. servus domino respondit equos ab hostibus captos esse.
6. diu credebam regem ab his interfectum esse.
7. frater mihi dixit exercitum prima luce profectum esse.
8. rex nuntiavit omnes naves tempestate saeva deletas esse.
9. dux nuntiavit tres milites e manibus hostium effugisse.
10. quis nesciebat principem profectum esse?

Personal pronouns in indirect speech

In direct speech the personal pronoun as subject is generally concealed in the verb itself. Thus discessi = I departed. Here the pronoun ego is not normally written; the ending **-i** tells us it is the 1st person singular.

However if we put **discessi** into indirect speech, we have to add the pronoun:

dicit me discessi.
He says that I have left.

Similarly discessisti = you left becomes dicit te discessisse = He says that you have left.

The pronouns can be strengthened by the addition of **ipse** in the accusative.

pater dicebat me ipsum has res fecisse.
My father used to say that I myself had done these things.

If the speaker is the same as the person who has carried ou the action, then **se** is used.

dominus dixit se ipsum illos servos liberavisse.
The master said that he himself had freed those slaves.

However, if the he / she / they is someone other than the he /she / they of the main verb, we should use eum / eam / eos /eas.

regina eam advenisse dixit.
The queen said that she (someone else) had arrived.

Negative indirect statements

In translating 'He says that the general has not arrived', Latin does not use dico followed by non, but instead **nego -are -avi -atum** = I say that … not'. Thus

negat ducem advenisse. He says that the general has arrived.

Exercise 17.2 Translate into English

1. negavi me hanc rem pessimam gessisse.
2. quis te muros delevisse nuntiavit?
3. militesne vobis se has res malas fecisse dixerunt?
4. num iuvenes se a pueris parvis superatos esse nuntiaverunt?
5. servus mihi saepe dicebat se aurum domini invenire conari.
6. milites negabant se multam fidem in duce novo habere.
7. cives clamabant se omnes spes in principe novo ponere.
8. custos negavit eum effugisse.
9. parentes scripserunt se in portu manere.
10. cur te ipsum hoc fecisse dicis?

Exercise 17.3 Translate into English

1. pueri negaverunt se has res pessimas fecisse.
2. quis vos oppidum oppugnavisse nuntiavit?
3. num dux vobis se has res malas fecisse dixit?
4. nonne iuvenes se pueros superavisse nuntiaverunt?
5. pueri mali nobis saepe dicebant se animalia vulnerare conari.
6. milites dixerunt se omnem fidem in rege novo habere.
7. socii magna voce clamaverunt se bellum novum cum hostibus gerere velle.
8. custodes negaverunt eos fugisse.
9. poeta scripsit se in portu Romae manere.
10. cur te ipsum hanc rem malam fecisse dicunt?

Exercise 17.4 Translate into Latin

1. The boy said that he had not done this.
2. Who announced that the army had left?
3. The guards said that they had seen the enemy.
4. I said that I had seen my friend in the city.
5. O brother, you did say that our father was in Rome, didn't you?
6. I didn't believe that all the arrows and spears had been handed over.
7. The sailors were shouting that almost all the ships had been destroyed by the storm.
8. Who said that the woman had been saved?
9. The messenger announced that all the slaves had escaped.
10. The general told the citizens that the city was no longer safe.

Chapter 18   Pluperfect subjunctive, active and passive

The **pluperfect subjunctive active** is formed by taking the perfect stem and adding the following endings:

-issem, -isses, -isset, -issemus, -issetis, -issent

amavissem	monuissem	rexissem	audivissem	cepissem	fuissem
amavisses	monuisses	rexisses	audivisses	cepisses	fuisses
amavisset	monuisset	rexisset	audivisset	cepisset	fuisset
amavissemus	monuissemus	rexissemus	audivissemus	cepissemus	fuissemus
amavissetis	monuissetis	rexissetis	audivissetis	cepissetis	fuissetis
amavissent	monuissent	rexissent	audivissent	cepissent	fuissent

The **pluperfect subjunctive** of the **passive** voice and **deponent** verbs is formed by taking the PPP + essem, esses, esset, essemus, essetis, essent

amatus essem	monitus essem	rectus essem	auditus essem	captus essem
amatus esses	monitus esses	rectus esses	auditus esses	captus esses
amatus esset	monitus esset	rectus esset	auditus esset	captus esset
amati essemus	moniti essemus	recti essemus	auditi essemus	capti essemus
amati essetis	moniti essetis	recti essetis	auditi essetis	capti essetis
amati essent	moniti essent	recti essent	auditi essent	capti essent

Instead of **ubi** or **postquam**, meaning **when** or **after**, we can use **cum + pluperfect subjunctive**

miles, cum ducem iratum esse vidisset, quam celerrime fugit.
When the soldier had seen that the general was angry, he fled as quickly as possible.

Exercise 18.1 Translate into English

1. senes, cum iuvenes conspexissent, ad montes fugerunt.
2. cum iter longissimum fecissetis, magnopere fessi eratis.
3. cum fortiter pugnavissetis, nec a rege nec a duce laudati estis.
4. dux, cum omnes milites sui fugissent, hostibus se tradidit.
5. discipulus, cum librum poetae clari legisset, alium legere voluit.
6. rex, cum verba nuntii audivisset, maxime timuit.
7. regem, cum somnus eum cepisset, custos statim gladio occidit.
8. milites huius exercitus, cum fortiter in proelio pugnavissent, praemia plurima acceperunt.
9. dux milites miseros, cum periculum effugissent, saevissime punivit.
10. senes, cum vinum optimum bibissent, somnus tandem cepit.

Exercise 18.2 Translate into English

1. hostes, cum nostros milites validos conspexissent, ad mare statim fugerunt.
2. cum iter longum fecissemus, magnopere fessi eramus.
3. copiae, cum diu pugnavissent, neque a regina neque a duce laudati sunt.
4. Graeci, cum Troiam delevissent, ad patriam redierunt.
5. discipuli, cum librum poetae mali legissent, alium legere noluerunt.
6. magister, cum haec verba audivisset, magnopere risit.
7. equus, cum multum cibi consumpsisset, statim fugit.
8. dux, cum de periculo monitus esset, aliam viam legit.
9. interea milites, cum omnis cibus in oppidum latus esset, fugerunt.
10. ceteris incolis, cum omnia tela ad urbem lata essent, non iam arma erant.

Exercise 18.3 Translate into Latin

1. When the general had warned the citizens about the danger, the young men laughed.
2. After the soldiers had brought the weapons into the town, they quickly departed.
3. When they had caught sight of the beautiful girls, the young men were very happy.
4. When they had heard their daughters' voices, the parents laughed.
5. When he had freed the slaves, everyone praised the master.
6. After giving the prize to the best boy, the teacher encouraged all the pupils to work.
7. When he had seen the fierce animals, the old man was very scared.
8. When he had received very severe wounds, the soldier soon died.
9. After seeing the boys in the street, the father hurried home.
10. After reading this excellent book, I wanted to read another one.

Chapter 19   cum + the imperfect subjunctive

cum + the imperfect subjunctive is a very common construction, where **cum** can mean 'when', 'while', 'because' 'since' or even 'although', depending upon the context.

milites nostri, cum hostes urbem oppugnarent, multa tela iaciebant.

While the enemy were attacking the city, our soldiers were throwing many weapons.

Exercise 19.1 Translate into English

1. discipuli, cum libros legerent, ridebant.
2. milites, cum hostes lente appropinquarent, fugere parabant.
3. pueri, cum hoc iter difficile esse sciebant, proficisci nolebant.
4. hic puer, cum parvus esset, cum eis iuvenibus validos pugnare nolebat.
5. hic puer fortis, cum minimus esset, cum illis iuvenibus pugnare parabat.
6. illum principem, cum nec fortis nec validus esset, nemo amavit.
7. naves, cum venti saevi essent, tempestate ad insulam pulsae sunt.
8. cum servi celeriter cucurrerent, nemo eos capere poterat.
9. servus, cum perterritus esset, fugere tandem constituit.
10. pater pueri, cum magnopere iratus esset, ad magistrum statim iit.

Exercise 19.2 Translate into English

1. pueri, cum libros legerent, non ridebant.
2. comites, cum amicus appropinquaret, in media via steterunt.
3. dux illam domum, cum pericula adesse credebat, ingredi nolebat.
4. hoc templum, cum pulcherrimum et sacerrimum esset, hostes deleverunt.
5. dominus, cum servus semper bene laboraret, eum magnopere laudabat.
6. illae naves, cum ventis saevis pellerentur, in portum ingredi potuerunt.
7. exercitus, cum hostes adessent, ad mare progressus est.
8. agricola, cum in agris laboraret, equos non vidit.
9. milites audaces, cum fortiter in proelio pugnarent, multa et saeva vulnera acceperunt.
10. duae ex his navibus, cum ad portum lente navigarent, tempestate saeva deletae sunt.

Exercise 19.3 Translate into Latin

1. My father was very angry as we were shouting.
2. Since the enemy were advancing quickly, the citizens decided to flee.
3. Because the master used to punish his slaves severely, his sons were very sad.
4. Because the enemy had defeated our army, the citizens no longer had faith in the leader.
5. As the storm was very fierce, the sailors prepared to defend themselves.
6. While the farmers were working in the fields, they saw an animal walking across the river.
7. While the sailors were preparing their ships, a violent storm suddenly arrived.
8. While we were sailing to that island, we caught sight of the king's ship.
9. While they animals were being driven into the town cente, they were making loud cries.
10. Since the master was very cruel, the slaves made up their minds to flee.

Vocabulary by Chapter

Chapter 1

interea	meanwhile	nec ... nec	neither nor	superbus	proud
lente	slowly	paene	almost	telum	weapon

Chapter 3

annus	year	fides	faith	res	thing, matter
dies	day	mensis	month	res publica	republic
domus	house	nox	night	spes	hope

Chapter 4

animal	animal	labor	task, work	princeps	chief, prince
custos	guard	opus	task, work	somnus	sleep
gens	people, tribe	praemium	prize, reward	tempestas	storm

Chapter 6

cogo	I force	custodio	I guard	peto	I seek, attack
contendo	I hurry, march	interficio	I kill	relinquo	I leave
convenio	I meet	iuvo	I help		
credo	I believe, trust	pello	I drive		

Chapter 7

fero	I carry	qui, quae, quod	who, which	totus	all

Chapter 8

alius	other	dum	while	ipse	self
celer	quick	idem	the same		

Chapter 12

impero	I order	persuadeo	I persuade

Chapter 15

conor	I try	loquor	I speak	proficiscor	I set out
egredior	I leave	morior	I die	progredior	I advance
hortor	I encourage	patior	I suffer		
ingedior	I enter	sequor	I follow		

Chapter 16

exercitus	army	portus	harbour	scio	I know
manus	hand	nescio	I don't know		

Answers to selected Exercises

Exercise 1.7
1. These wretched boys are wounded by the savage weapons.
2. Almost all the pupils are praised by the proud teacher.
3. Almost all the books are read by a few boys.
4. Meanwhile the rest of the ships are destroyed by the savage winds.
5. A few slaves are often punished by the bad master.
6. This very good wine is slowly drunk by the new sailors.
7. The Greek sailors are overcome by the Roman soldiers.
8. That horse seems to be sleeping.
9. That tired enemy are being killed by the weapons of the Romans.
10. We are neither captured nor wounded by the angry soldiers.

Exercise 1.7E
1. The very beautiful Helen is captured by Paris.
2. This large city is bravely defended by the Trojans.
3. These brave men are neither killed nor wounded by the Greeks.
4. This huge horse is built by the strong Greeks.
5. The very wretched Helen is finally freed by the very brave Menelaus.
6. The tired Trojans are easily overcome by these very strong Greeks.
7. A lot of gold is captured by those happy Greeks.
8. All the ships of the Greeks seem to be leaving.
9. After the battle a lot of wine is drunk by the tired Greeks.
10. Almost all the weapons are thrown by the cruel enemy.

Exercise 2.2
1. The very beautiful Helen was being captured by Paris.
2. The small city was being bravely defended by all the citizens.
3. The Roman soldiers were not being overcome by the tired enemy.
4. Meanwhile a huge horse was being built by the Greeks.
5. The lucky wife was being finally freed by her brave husband.
6. The Trojans were being beaten by the Greeks.
7. A lot of wine was being taken by the lucky Greeks.
8. The land was finally being caught sight of by the happy sailors.
9. After the battle this food was being eaten by our soldiers.
10. Many weapons were being thrown by the very wild enemy.

Exercise 2.2E
1. The slave seemed to be working.
2. All the pupils were being praised by the wise teachers.
3. Almost all the books were being read by all the boys.
4. The rest of the ships were being destroyed by the savage wind.
5. A few slaves were often punished by the bad queen.
6. The best wine was always drunk by the sailors.
7. The Greek sailors were being beaten by bold soldiers.
8. The wretched horse was being wounded by bad slaves.
9. All the enemy were being killed with swords by the cruel soldiers.
10. The slaves were neither punished nor praised by the proud noble master.

Exercise 3.2
1. The miserable girls will not be wounded by the savage soldiers.
2. Almost all the pupils will be praised tomorrow by the wise teachers.
3. Those books will be read in three months by all the boys.
4. The rest of the ships will be destroyed by a savage storm within five days.
5. A few slaves will be punished by the bad queen on the third day.
6. The soldiers will remain for many hours in the town.
7. The Greek sailors will be beaten by the brave soldiers within two hours.
8. The wretched horses will be captured by the bad slaves.
9. The guards will be killed by the cruel soldiers with swords within three hours.
10. The good slaves will not be punished by the noble master.

Exercise 3.2E

1. The slaves will be led back to Rome within two days.
2. The small city will be defended for two years by the brave citizens.
3. The Roman soldiers will be neither overcome nor wounded by the tired enemy.
4. The huge horse will be built by the Greeks within six days.
5. The lucky wife will be freed by her brave husband within three hours.
6. The Trojans will be overcome by the bold Greeks on the second night.
7. A lot of gold will be taken by the lucky Greeks.
8. The island will be caught sight of tomorrow by the happy sailors.
9. After the battle all the food will be eaten by the soldiers.
10. Many arrows will be thrown by our soldiers.

Exercise 4.2

1. After the battle the tired chief wanted to sleep.
2. All the animals will be killed by the savage storm.
3. All the people wanted to put their hope in the chief.
4. All the people of Greece wanted to fight with the Trojans.
5. The Romans managed the republic for a long time.
6. We have been able to overcome the enemy by the effort of all the citizens.
7. Although the task was difficult, the slaves worked well for many hours.
8. 'Have faith in me!' shouted the leader.
9. Although they had drunk a lot of wine, the soldiers were not able to go to sleep.
10. The tribes of Britain were often fighting each other.

Exercise 4.2E

1. Before the battle the chief had great hope of victory.
2. Quintus is a young man of great hope.
3. The Romans had faith in the republic for a long time.
4. The people put faith in the brave chief.
5. Three guards were drinking in front of the wall.
6. We put all our hopes in the strong leader.
7. The soldiers always had hope of saving the animals.
8. We have great hope of overcoming the enemy.
9. The old man will soon fall asleep because the task is long and difficult.
10. Defeating the enemy will be a matter of great work (i.e. require a lot of effort)

Exercise 7.1

1. The wind carries the storm into the city.
2. The pupils used to bring books to the teacher.
3. The slaves will bring prizes to the king.
4. The husband brought gifts for his wife.
5. The leader had already brought all the weapons.

Exercise 7.1E

1. The winds bring the storms in to the town.
2. The pupil used to bring three books to the teacher.
3. The son will bring a prize to the king.
4. The boy's father brought many gifts to the teacher.
5. The chief had already brought all the swords.

Exercise 7.3

1. The man, who was tired, did not want to work.
2. Almost the whole city was destroyed in the war.
3. The whole place in which the boys are playing is very beautiful.
4. This part of the town which all the citizens love is very beautiful.
5. I gave many gifts to that woman, whose daughter is very beautiful.
6. I often saw that boy, whom the teacher punished, in the town with his friends.
7. O slave, bring these books to the teacher who is in the town now.
8. Did you see the young man I fought with yesterday?
9. The enemy with whom the Romans fought quickly escaped.
10. These are the girls with whom I often used to play.

Exercise 7.3E

1. The troops who were very tired did not want to fight.
2. Those books which the poet wrote are very beautiful.
3. The place in which the girls were playing is very beautiful.
4. This is the town which few citizens like.
5. I used to give many gifts to the man whose daughters are very beautiful.
6. I caught sight of the boys, whom the teacher punished, in the middle of the city.
7. Boys, bring these books to the teacher who is sleeping in the country-house.
8. Companions, did you see the young men with whom I fought yesterday?
9. The young men with whom the soldiers fought fled.
10. These are the weapons with which I often used to fight.

Exercise 7.5

1. We do not like those who praise the king.
2. Don't believe those who say these things!
3. That which is difficult often brings rewards.
4. Those young men always watch those women who are very beautiful.
5. We were not able to capture those who were running quickly.

Exercise 8.1

1. While I was hurrying into the city, I caught sight of the other soldiers.
2. While the master was working in the villa, the slaves took all the swift horses.
3. Meanwhile, the leader left the other troops on the mountain.
4. The king himself took the dinner to his wife.
5. While the slaves were sleeping, the maids were preparing dinner.
6. Some woman were laughing, others were sleeping.
7. I myself drove the same animals in to the field yesterday.
8. While the guards were playing, almost all the slaves escaped.
9. While my friend was helping me, another animal escaped.
10. Some soldiers were killed, others received savage wounds.

Exercise 8.1E

1. Meanwhile, while the leader was hurrying to town, the other soldiers departed.
2. Almost all the slaves fled quickly while the master was working in the villa.
3. The leader left the other soldiers near the river.
4. The king himself neither drank the wine nor ate the food.
5. While the slaves were driving the animals into the field, the queen suddenly came out of the villa.
6. Some men were eating, others were drinking.
7. I saw the king himself in the street yesterday.
8. These things were carried out on the same day.
9. The storm often comes at the same hour.
10. The swift young men were able to capture almost all the animals.

Exercise 9.1

1. When the lucky slaves had been freed by the noble master they were happy.
2. When the soldier had been made leader by his companions he behaved arrogantly.
3. When the old men had been left behind by all their companions, they escaped as quickly as possible.
4. When the proud king had been warned about the danger by his companions he resolved to behave himself.
5. Tomorrow I shall destroy this wall built by the slaves.
6. The soldiers wounded by by the enemy will guard the walls.
7. The general greatly praised the soldiers killed in battle.
8. The wretched slaves ordered to work by their master immediately fled.
9. Almost all the citizens, who had been wounded by the enemy, fled from the city.
10. The town that had been attacked for a long time was finally taken.

Exercise 9.1E

1. The wind drove the ship that had been destroyed by the storm to the island.
2. For a long time the farmer looked for the animals that had been left in the field.
3. The chief immediately took all the weapons that had been taken to the town.
4. The proud queen who had been warned by her daughter immediately fled.
5. These temples that were built within two months have been destroyed quickly by the storm.
6. The enemy destroyed the walls that were bravely guarded by the enemy.
7. The soldiers who had been defeated in battle finally went to sleep.

8. The huge horse that had been left near the walls was brought into the city.
9. The ships that had been destroyed neither by the winds nor the storms finally reached Britain.
10. I read the other books that had been praised by the teacher within three days.

Exercise 10.1
1. The chief caught sight of almost all the soldiers leaving the town.
2. The boy was laughing as he looked at the prizes.
3. The very bad men were laughing as they took our money.
4. The citizens loved the chief who behaved properly.
5. The boys were safe as they slept in the country-house.
6. The leader praised the soldiers who were guarding the temple for the whole night.
7. As the sailors were shouting they were taken to the ship.
8. The soldiers were killed as they fought bravely in the fierce battle.
9. The mother caught sight of her sons as they played in the street.
10. The general forced the fleeing soldiers to return.

Exercise 10.1E
1. The guard caught sight of all the people as they rushed into the town.
2. The boys were terrified as they watched the savage storm.
3. The evil young men were laughing as they took all the gold.
4. The citizens drove out from the city the king who was behaving badly.
5. The girls were not safe as they slept in the country-house.
6. The king praised the guards who remained the whole night on the wall.
7. As the people were shouting bravely they were led to the king.
8. All the leaders who were fighting bravely were finally killed.
9. The brother caught sight of his sister as she played in the street.
10. The father saw his son as he slept in the field.

Exercise 11.1
1. The citizens hurried to the centre of the city in order to see the queen.
2. The Romans fought bravely to defeat the enemy.
3. The slaves quickly escaped in order not to be punished by their master.
4. The young men drove the animals into the field in order to kill them there.
5. The soldiers assembled in the town in order to choose another leader.
6. The soldiers immediately fled in order not to be captured by the enemy.
7. The citizens left the city as quickly as possible to escape from the enemy.
8. The people built a huge wall to defend the city.
9. The boy went to the town with his father so as not to be on his own in the country-house.
10. All the weapons were taken into the city in order that the citizens could defend themselves.

Exercise 11.1E
1. The king hurried to the middle of the town to see his companion.
2. The citizens quickly assembled to catch sight of the new slaves.
3. The enemy quickly fled so as not to be beaten by us.
4. The farmers drove the other animals from the town so that the citizens would not be terrified.
5. The same soldiers hurried to town to see the leader again.
6. The guards immediately fled so as not to be killed by the enemy.
7. Almost all the citizens left the city to escape the enemy.
8. The soldiers used to eat a lot of good food to have strong bodies.
9. The girl remained in the country-house to be on her own.
10. All the spears and arrows were taken to the town so that the leader could defend himself.

Exercise 11.3
1. The father sent his son to Rome to work with his brother there.
2. The leader ordered the best soldiers to hurry to the city to defend it bravely.
3. The teacher showed the best books to the pupils so that they would write better.
4. The master praised the slave in order that he run more quickly.
5. The leader said these words to the soldiers in order that they fight more boldly.
6. The king himself arrived at the city in order that the soldiers defend the walls more bravely.
7. The king sent the soldiers to the fields in order that the farmers could work more safely.
8. The leader sent the soldiers to the town to destroy the walls.
9. The father punished his son very harshly in order that he should work better.
10. The leader handed over the best weapons to the soldiers in order that they carry out the matter more easily.

Exercise 12.1

1. The wise teacher warned the pupils to read the best books.
2. My father asked the same young men to leave the middle of the city.
3. Surely the citizens didn't order you to throw the animals into the river?
4. The chief himself persuaded all the soldiers to stay in the city.
5. Surely the leader asked you to defend the city?
6. Why did the chief order you to cross the river?
7. Who ordered you to drive the animals into the field?
8. The leader ordered the bold soldiers to charge against the enemy at the third hour.
9. The teacher persuaded the pupils to behave themselves.
10. The angry king asked the slave to prepare the weapons.

Exercise 12.1E

1. The father advised his son not to read the very bad books.
2. The guard asked the same soldiers to leave the middle of the town.
3. Surely the leader ordered you to attack the town?
4. The queen herself persuaded her son to stay in the city.
5. Surely the king ordered you to remain in the city?
6. Why did the guard order you to throw yourself in the river?
7. Who ordered you take the food to the animals?
8. The master ordered the slaves to prepare food for the horses.
9. The teacher persuaded the boys to write well.
10. The king asked the slave to prepare the weapons.

Exercise 14.1

1. The king didn't want to be heard by the soldiers.
2. The shouts cannot be heard.
3. The citizens don't want to be captured.
4. The animals couldn't be forced into the field.
5. The animals didn't want to be collected.
6. The woman didn't want to be caught sight of.
7. The leader ordered this food to be eaten.
8. The leader ordered the walls to be bravely guarded.
9. The king had ordered the city to be defended.
10. The chief won't order the city to be destroyed.
11. The animal didn't want to be led along the road.
12. The leader immediately ordered war to be waged with the enemy.
13. These spears cannot be thrown into the town.
14. The gold will not be able to be found.
15. The leader ordered the slaves to be killed.
16. The teacher ordered all the books to be read.
17. The leader ordered the messenger to be sent to Rome.
18. The master will order the slave to be killed.
19. The leader didn't want the gold to be shown to the king.
20. The animal didn't want to be put in that place.
21. The horse doesn't want to be driven by the boy.
22. The king ordered the gold to be looked for in that place.
23. The horses didn't want to be led back to the city.
24. The Romans didn't want to be ruled by kings any longer.
25. The boys didn't want to be left behind in Rome.
26. The poet didn't want this book to be written.

Exercise 15.1

1. He was encouraging his mother to leave.
2. The leader left at the third hour.
3. The Romans will enter the war within two years.
4. The old men spoke for two hours.
5. Nine soldiers died in the battle.
6. For a long time we endured the savage cries of the animals.
7. We followed the old men for three hours.
8. The soldiers will set off within two hours.
9. The enemy troops go forward slowly.
10. I shall set off within four days.

Exercise 15.1E
1. The father encouraged the son to work at once.
2. The soldiers will leave on the second hour.
3. The fourth farmer will go into the villa within two hours.
4. The angry women spoke for two hours.
5. The queen died suddenly in the villa.
6. The parents endured the savage cries of the little girls for the whole day.
7. We followed the swift men for three hours.
8. The leader will set out to the mountains within two hours.
9. Almost all the troops went forward to the river.
1 0. The king will try to set out on a long journey within three days.

Exercise 15.3
1. We heard the leader encouraging the soldiers.
2. Boy, help the slave who is trying to carry out his task.
3. We caught sight of the soldiers as they left the town.
4. We escaped from the women who were speaking in the villa.
5. As the troops set out to the mountain almost all the citizens were sleeping.
6. As the enemy tried to escape the Roman leader resolved to attack the town.
7. Don't believe the men saying these things.
8. The enemy suddenly charged the troops as they set out.
9. The son greeted the father as he went in.
10. The guards drove away the men as they went forward to the town.

Exercise 15.4
1. After suffering many wounds the soldier finally died.
2. After he had often tried to escape but in vain, the soldier decided to stay.
3. After the old men had spoken for many hours they finally left the house.
4. After the soldiers had set out on the long journey they were now very tired.
5. After the troops had set out at first light they reached the river within three hours.
6. After the young men had followed the men across the mountains they finally caught sight of them near the river.
7. The master severely punished the boy who had tried to take the prizes.
8. The soldiers led back the man who had suffered many harsh things.
9. Our soldiers charged the enemy who had tried to attack the town.
10. The crowd of women who had set out from the city at first light walked for five hours.

Exercise 15.5
1. This man never heard the queen encouraging the soldiers.
2. The crowd of young men setting out from the town at first light walked for three hours.
3. Boys, help the old man trying to do his own task.
4. The men killed almost all the soldiers who had been trying to attack the city.
5. The leader caught sight of the people as they went out of the city.
6. The teacher very savagely the boys who had tried to destroy the prizes.
7. The boys escaped from the young men speaking in the street.
8. The sailors finally caught sight of the young men in the island after following them across the sea.
9. As the soldiers set out to the river almost all the citizens remained in the centre of the city.
10. After the women had set out at first light they reached the river within a few hours.
11. As the enemy troops were trying to escape the Greek leader resolved to attack the city.
12. The soldiers who had advanced three hours before quickly reached the place.
13. Don't believe the boy who is saying these things!
14. The married pair returned home after speaking for many hours.
15. The soldiers attacked the men with large weapons as they were setting out.
16. After trying to drive the animal but in vain, the maid returned to the country-house.
17. The daughter greeted her mother as she was going into the temple.
18. After the soldiers had endured many harsh things they finally died.
19. The guard drove the man with weapons as he was advancing to the town.
20. As he followed the young man the swift soldier was killed by the weapon.

Exercise 16.1

1. I know that the teacher's house is small.
2. The poet writes that the chief reigns well.
3. Do you believe the king is in the island?
4. I hear that the army is in the city.
5. All the citizens say the enemy is approaching.
6. The leader always answers that the soldiers don't know these things.
7. The old man is shouting that the soldiers are leaving.
8. Do you know that the enemy army is in the harbour?
9. The king hears that the gold is no longer in the country-house.
10. Very many men say that the queen's hands are beautiful.

Exercise 16.2

1. Who knew that the men were at home?
2. The poet narrated that the chief ruled well.
3. Did you used to believe that Rome was an island?
4. I heard that the army was advancing towards the city.
5. All the citizens were saying that the enemy were setting out.
6. The proud leader always used to reply that his soldiers didn't know these things.
7. The old man shouted that the soldiers were leaving.
8. Did you know that the enemy army was advancing to the harbour?
9. The king announced that the city was now in the hands of the enemy.
10. Very men said that the king had very small hands.

Exercise 17.1

1. The messenger says that the enemy have taken the city.
2. The brother announced that the harbour had been captured by the enemy.
3. Almost all the citizens now know that the chief has died.
4. All the pupils didn't know that the teacher had written a very famous book.
5. The salve replied to the master that the horses had been captured by the enemy.
6. For a long time I used to believe the king had been killed by these men.
7. The brother told me that the army had set out at first light.
8. The king announced that all the ships had been destroyed by the savage storm.
9. The leader announced that three soldiers had escaped from the hands of the enemy.
10. Who didn't know that the chief had set out?

Exercise 17.2

1. I said that I had not done this very bad thing.
2. Who announced that you had destroyed the walls?
3. Did the soldiers tell you that they had done the bad things?
4. Surely the young men didn't announce that they had had overcome by the small boys?
5. The slave often used to tell me that he was trying to find the master's gold.
6. The soldiers used to say that they didn't have a lot of faith in the new chief.
7. The citizens were shouting that that they were putting all their hopes in the new chief.
8. The guard said that man had not escaped.
9. The parents wrote that they were staying in the harbour.
10. Why do you say that you did this?

Exercise 17.3

1. The boys said that they had not done these very bad things.
2. Who announced that you had attacked the town?
3. Surely the leader didn't tell you that he had done these bad things?
4. Surely the young men announced that they had overcome the boys?
5. The naughty boys often used to tell us that they were trying to wound the animals.
6. The soldiers said that they had every faith in the new king.
7. The allies shouted in a loud voice that they wanted to wage a new war with the enemy.
8. The guards said that those men had not escaped.
9. The poet wrote that they were staying in the port of Rome.
10. Why are they saying that you yourself have done this bad thing?

Exercise 18.1

1. When the old men had seen the young men they fled to the mountains.
2. When you had made the very long journey you were very tired.
3. After you had fought bravely, you were praised by neither the king nor the leader.
4. When all his soldiers had fled, the leader handed himself over to the enemy.
5. When he had read the book of the famous poet, the pupil wanted to read another one.
6. When he had heard the words of the messenger, the king was very afraid.
7. The guard immediately killed with a sword the king after he had fallen asleep.
8. After the soldiers of this army had fought bravely in the battle received very many prizes.
9. The leader very savagely punished the wretched soldiers after they had escaped from the danger.
10. After they had drunk the very good wine, the old men finally went to sleep.

Exercise 18.2

1. When they had caught sight of our strong soldiers, the enemy immediately fled to the sea.
2. When we had made the long journey, we were very tired.
3. When they had fought for a long time, the troops were praised by neither the queen nor the general.
4. When they had destroyed Troy, the Greeks returned to Greece.
5. When they had read the book of the bad poet the pupils didn't want to read another one.
6. When he had heard these words, the teacher laughed a lot.
7. When he had eaten a lot of food the horse immediately fled.
8. When he had been warned about the danger, the leader chose another road.
9. Meanwhile the soldiers fled when all the food had been brought into the town.
10. When all the weapons had been taken to the city, the rest of the inhabitants no longer had any weapons.

Exercise 19.1

1. As they were reading the books, the pupils were laughing.
2. As the enemy were approaching slowly, the soldiers were preparing to flee.
3. As they knew that this journey was difficult, the boys didn't want to set out.
4. As he was small, this boy didn't want to fight with those strong young men.
5. Although he was very small, this brave boy was preparing to fight with those young men.
6. Nobody loved that chief as he was neither brave nor strong.
7. As the winds were wild, the ships were driven to the island by the storm.
8. As the slaves ran quickly, no one was able to capture them.
9. As he was terrified, the slave finally resolved to flee.
10. As he was very angry, the boy's father went immediately to the teacher.

Exercise 19.2

1. As they read the books, the boys were not laughing.
2. As the friend was approaching, the companions stood in the middle of the street.
3. The leader did not want to enter that house, as he believed there were dangers there.
4. The enemy destroyed this temple, as it was very beautiful and sacred.
5. The master often greatly praised the slave, as he always worked well.
6. Although they were being driven by the wild winds, those ships were able to enter the harbour.
7. As the enemy were present, the army advanced to the sea.
8. As he was working in the fields, the farmer didn't see the horses.
9. As they were fighting bravely in the battle, the bold soldiers received many savage wounds.
10. As they sailed slowly to the harbour, two of the ships were destroyed by the wild storm.

Scholarship Papers
Nero takes advantage of a city fire

hoc anno in urbe Romanorum incendium ingens fuit. ortum est in paucis tabernis, sed mox flammae magnam partem urbis deleverunt. cives, periculo perterriti, ex urbe quam celerrime effugerunt. Nero, qui tum princeps erat, forte Roma aberat; sine mora rediit ut auxilium civibus ferret. urbs Roma, quae maxima pulcherrimaque fuerat, paene incendio deleta est. postea, ubi Nero imperavit ut urbem reficerent, villam novam et pulcherrimam sibi quoque aedificaverunt. plurimi tamen cives Neroni non credebant. 'incendium ab Nerone factum est. cives ab principe interfecti sunt.'

Nero igitur, vir crudelissimus, Christianos punire constituit quamquam nihil fecerant: alii ab animalibus occisi sunt, alii vivi incensi sunt. Neronem tamen cives non amabant, et paucis post annis milites eum ex urbe expulerunt; tandem in villa prope Romam princeps se occidit.

Proper Nouns	**Vocabulary**
Nero, Neronis Nero	incendium -i, n. a fire
Christianus, -i a Christian	ortum est 'it arose'
	taberna -ae, f. shop
	flamma -ae, f. flame
	reficio -ere I rebuild
	incendio -ere, incensi, incensum I set on fire

Julius Caesar is captured by pirates

Caesar olim ab urbe Roma fugiebat et trans mare cum paucis amicis in parva nave navigabat. subito piratae, quorum illo tempore multi erant in omnibus maris partibus, eos captos ad parvam insulam duxerunt. hic Caesarem captivum tenebant. ubi pretium quinquaginta talentorum pro vita eius rogaverunt, Caesar amicos suos Romam miserunt ut hanc pecuniam sibi ferrent. simulatque amici redierunt, pretium promissum ferentes, Caesar liberatus in aliam insulam missus est. ibi statim naves paravit ut ad illam insulam in qua captivus fuerat rediret. ubi piratas oppugnatos facile cepit, non solum quinquaginta talenta quae habebant sibi rapuit. tum homines ipsos crudelissime punivit et, iam multo divitior quam antea, Romam rediit.

Proper Names	**Vocabulary**
Caesar Caesaris m. Caesar	pirata -ae m. pirate
Roma Romae f. Rome	tempus temporis n. time
	captivus captivi m. prisoner
	pretium pretii n. price, ransom
	vita -ae f. life
	simulatque as soon as
	promitto promittere promisi promissus I promise
	recipio recipere recepi receptus I recover
	rapio rapere rapui raptus I seize
	multo much
	dives divitis rich
	antea before

Scipio frees a prisoner

ubi urbs ingens in <u>Hispania</u> a <u>Romanis</u> oppugnata erat, <u>captiva</u> ad <u>Scipionem</u> ducta est, puella pulcherrima quae <u>oculos</u> omnium ad se <u>vertebat</u>; ea a principe <u>Hispano</u>, qui iuvenis erat, amabatur. ubi Scipio eam vidit, statim servo imperavit ut et <u>parentes</u> eius et illum principem Hispanum ad se duceret, iuvenique 'ego,' inquit 'iuvenis sum et illa puella pulchra mihi etiam cara est. quod tamen tua est, tutam eam tibi trado. mihi <u>satis</u> magnum <u>praemium</u> erit, si tu mihi <u>populoque</u> Romano amicus eris. hoc etiam credere <u>debes</u>: multi mihi <u>similes</u> in urbe Roma sunt nec <u>ullum</u> populum invenire poteris qui Hispanis <u>magis</u> amicus esse vult quam Romani.' princeps magno <u>gaudio</u> motus est et <u>Scipionem</u> adiit ut <u>dextram</u> eius teneret.

Proper names	Vocabulary
Hispania -ae Spain	captiva -ae f. prisoner
Romanus -i Roman	oculus -i m. eye
Scipio -onis Scipio (Roman general)	verto -ere verti versus I turn
Hispanus -a -um Spanish	parens -entis m./ f. parent
Roma -ae Rome	satis enough
	praemium -i n. reward
	populus -i m. people
	debeo -ere debui debitus I ought
	similis -e similar
	ullus -a -um any
	magis more
	gaudium -i n. joy
	dextra -ae f. right hand

Julius Caesar is assassinated

<u>Gallia</u> victa, <u>Iulius Caeasar</u> erat vir <u>potentissimus</u> Romanorum. ille a Britannia ad Africam regebat. multi tamen <u>coniurationem</u> contra Caesarem <u>incipere</u> cupiebat ut eum interficerent. illi dixerunt 'Caesare interfecto, mox nos ipsi regemus.' principes <u>coniurationis</u> erant <u>Brutus</u> et <u>Cassius</u> quibus <u>Caesar</u> diu credebat. itaque Brutus et Cassius amicis suis imperaverunt ut in foro convenirent.
<u>Caesar</u>, trans forum ambulans, magnam turbam <u>Romanorum</u> vidit. pauci virorum, qui in <u>curia</u> convenerant, <u>Caesarem</u> adierunt.
Caesar 'quid cupitis?' rogavit. deinde viros appropinquantes, qui gladios ferebant, vidit. Caesar clamavit 'estne hodie dies meae mortis?' <u>coniurati</u> <u>Caesarem</u> gladiis interfecerunt. antequam necatus est, <u>Caesar</u> <u>Brutum</u> inter hostes vidit. 'et tu, <u>Brute</u>? inquit et, his verbis dictis, periit. haec clara verba <u>extrema</u> <u>Iulii Casesaris</u> erant.

Proper Names	Vocabulary
Gallia -ae f. Gaul	potens -tis powerful
Iulius -i Caesar -is Julius Caesar	coniuratio -onis f. conspiracy
Brutus -i Brutus	curia -ae f. senate-house
Cassius -i Cassius	coniuratus -i conspirator
	extremus -a -um last

Scholarship Sentences

1. The leader ordered the soldiers to attack the town.
2. The city was soon captured by the enemy.
3. Why are you waiting near the big temple?

4. The leader's sister greatly loved her brother.
5. The shout was often heard in the middle of the night.
6. Why are the twenty soldiers not attacking the guards?

7. The leader's wife was fearing the angry mother.
8. Gold was given to the guards because of their loyalty.
9. Did you see sixteen soldiers yesterday?

10. Antonius greatly loved the beautiful queen.
11. It was easy for the soldiers to cross the river.
12. The slave was captured yesterday by chance.

13. The boys ran in order to see the queen.
14. The city has been captured by a hundred soldiers.
15. Do you want to walk into town?

16. The walls are being attacked by a thousand soldiers.
17. Why do you now not want to run with me?
18. The boys hurried in order to look at the body.

GRAMMAR SUMMARY

Nouns

Declension	1	2	2	2	2
Gender	feminine	masculine	masculine	masculine	neuter

Singular

Nominative.	puella	servus	puer	ager	bellum
Vocative	puella	serve	puer	ager	bellum
Accusative	puellam	servum	puerum	agrum	bellum
Genitive	puellae	servi	pueri	agri	belli
Dative	puellae	servo	puero	agro	bello
Ablative	puella	servo	puero	agro	bello

Plural

Nominative	puellae	servi	pueri	agri	bella
Vocative	puellae	servi	pueri	agri	bella
Accusative	puellas	servos	pueros	agros	bella
Genitive	puellarum	servorum	puerorum	agrorum	bellorum
Dative	puellis	servis	pueris	agris	bellis
Ablative	puellis	servis	pueris	agris	bellis

Declension	3	3	3 neut.	4	5

Singular

Nominative	rex	civis	nomen	exercitus	res
Vocative	rex	civis	nomen	exercitus	res
Accusative	regem	civem	nomen	exercitum	rem
Genitive	regis	civis	nominis	exercitus	rei
Dative	regi	civi	nomini	exercitui	rei
Ablative	rege	cive	nomine	exercitus	re

Plural

Nominative	reges	cives	nomina	exercitus	res
Vocative	reges	cives	nomina	exercitus	res
Accusative	reges	cives	nomina	exercitus	res
Genitive	regum	civium	nominum	exercituum	rerum
Dative	regibus	civibus	nominibus	exercitibus	rebus
Ablative	regibus	civibus	nominibus	exercitibus	rebus

Adjectives

bonus -a -um   good

	masculine	feminine	neuter
Singular			
Nominative	bonus	bona	bonum
Vocative	bone	bona	bonum
Accusative	bonum	bonam	bonum
Genitive	boni	bonae	boni
Dative	bono	bonae	bono
Ablative	bono	bona	bon
Plural			
Nominative	boni	bonae	bona
Vocative	boni	bonae	bona
Accusative	bonos	bonas	bonos
Genitive	bonorum	bonarum	bonorum
Dative	bonis	bonis	bonis
Ablative	bonis	bonis	bonis

miser -a -um   miserable

	masculine	feminine	neuter
Singular			
Nominative	miser	misera	miserum
Vocative	miser	misera	miserum
Accusative	miserum	miseram	miserum
Genitive	miseri	miserae	miseri
Dative	misero	miserae	misero
Ablative	misero	misera	misero
Plural			
Nominative	miseri	miserae	misera
Vocative	miseri	miserae	misera
Accusative	miseros	miseras	misera
Genitive	miserorum	miserarum	miserorum
Dative	miseris	miseris	miseris
Ablative	miseris	miseris	miseris

sacer -ra -rum   sacred

	masculine	feminine	neuter
Singular			
Nominative	sacer	sacra	sacrum
Vocative	sacer	sacra	sacrum
Accusative	sacrum	sacram	sacrum
Genitive	sacri	sacrae	sacri
Dative	sacro	sacrae	sacro
Ablative	sacro	sacra	sacro
Plural			
Nominative	sacri	sacrae	sacra
Vocative	sacri	sacrae	sacra
Accusative	sacros	sacras	sacros
Genitive	sacrorum	sacrarum	sacrorum
Dative	sacris	sacris	sacris
Ablative	sacris	sacris	sacris

laetior -ius happier

Singular

Nominative	laetior	laetior	laetius
Vocative	laetior	laetior	laetius
Accusative	laetiorem	laetiorem	laetius
Genitive	laetioris	laetioris	laetioris
Dative	laetiori	laetiori	laetiori
Ablative	laetiore	laetiore	laetiore

Plural

Nominative	laetiores	laetiores	laetiora
Vocative	laetiores	laetiores	laetiora
Accusative	laetiores	laetiores	laetiora
Genitive	laetiorum	laetiorum	laetiorum
Dative	laetioribus	laetioribus	laetioribus
Ablative	laetioribus	laetioribus	laetioribus

tristis, triste sad, gloomy

Singular

Nominative	tristis	tristis	triste
Vocative	tristis	tristis	triste
Accusative	tristem	tristem	triste
Genitive	tristis	tristis	tristis
Dative	tristi	tristi	tristi
Ablative	tristi	tristi	tristi

Plural

Nominative	tristes	tristes	tristia
Vocative	tristes	tristes	tristia
Accusative	tristes	tristes	tristia
Genitive	tristium	tristium	tristium
Dative	tristibus	tristibus	tristibus
Ablative	tristibus	tristibus	tristibus

ingens, ingens huge

Singular

Nominative	ingens	ingens	ingens
Vocative	ingens	ingens	ingens
Accusative	ingentem	ingentem	ingens
Genitive	ingentis	ingentis	ingentis
Dative	ingenti	ingenti	ingenti
Ablative	ingenti	ingenti	ingenti

Plural

Nominative	ingentes	ingentes	ingentia
Vocative	ingentes	ingentes	ingentia
Accusative	ingentes	ingentes	ingentia
Genitive	ingentium	ingentium	ingentium
Dative	ingentibus	ingentibus	ingentibus
Ablative	ingentibus	ingentibus	ingentibus

celer -is -e fast, swift

Nominative	celer	celeris	celere
Vocative	celer	celeris	celere
Accusative	celerem	celerem	celere
Genitive	celeris	celeris	celeris
Dative	celeri	celeri	celeri
Ablative	celeri	celeri	celeri

plural

nominative	celeres	celeres	celeria
vocative	celeres	celeres	celeria
accusative	celeres	celeres	celeria
genitive	celerum	celerum	celerum
dative	celeribus	celeribus	celeribus
ablative	celeribus	celeribus	celeribus

hic, haec, hoc   this

Singular

Nominative	hic	haec	hoc
Accusative	hunc	hanc	hoc
Genitive	huius	huius	huius
Dative	huic	huic	huic
Ablative	hoc	hac	hoc

Plural

Nominative	hi	hae	haec
Accusative	hos	has	haec
Genitive	horum	harum	horum
Dative	his	his	his
Ablative	his	his	his

ille, illa, illud = that

Singular

Nominative	ille	illa	illud
Accusative	illum	illam	illud
Genitive	illius	illius	illius
Dative	illi	illi	illi
Ablative	illo	illa	illo

Plural

Nominative	illi	illae	illa
Accusative	illos	illas	illa
Genitive	illorum	illarum	illorum
Dative	illis	illis	illis
Ablative	illis	illis	illis

is, ea, id   that; he she, it

Singular

Nominative	is	ea	id
Accusative	eum	eam	id
Genitive	eius	eius	eius
Dative	ei	ei	ei
Ablative	eo	eā	eo

Plural

Nominative	ei, ii	eae	ea
Accusative	eos	eas	ea
Genitive	eorum	earum	eorum
Dative	eis, iis	eis, iis	eis
Ablative	eis, iis	eis, iis	eis, iis

ipse ipsa ipsum   -self

singular

Nominative	ipse	ipsa	ipsum
Accusative	ipsum	ipsam	ipsum
Genitive	ipsius	ipsius	ipsius
dative	ipsi	ipsi	ipsi
Ablative	ipso	ipsa	ipso

plural

Nominative	ipsi	ipsae	ipsa
Accusative	ipsos	ipsas	ipsa
Genitive	ipsorum	ipsarum	ipsorum
Dative	ipsis	ipsis	ipsis
Ablative	ipsis	ipsis	ipsis

solus -a -um   alone

Nominative	solus	sola	solum
Accusative	solum	solam	solum
Genitive	solius	solius	solius
Dative	soli	soli	soli
Ablative	solo	sola	solo

unus -a -um   one

Nominative	unus	una	unum
Accusative	unum	unam	unum
Genitive	unius	unius	unius
Dative	uni	uni	uni
Ablative	uno	una	uno

totus -a -um   whole

singular

Nominative	totus	tota	totum
Accusative	totum	totam	totum
Genitive	totius	totius	totius
Dative	toti	toti	toti
Ablative	toto	tota	toto

plural

Nominative	toti	totae	tota
Accusative	totos	totas	tota
Genitive.	totorum	totarum	totorum
Dative	totis	totis	totis
Ablative	totis	totis	totis

alius -a -iud   other

singular

Nominative	alius	alia	aliud
Accusative	alium	aliam	aliud
Genitive	alius	alius	alius
Dative	alii	alii	alii
Ablative	alio	alia	alio

plural

Nominative	alii	aliae	alia
Accusative	alios	alias	alia
Genitive	aliorum	aliarum	aliorum
Dative	aliis	aliis	aliis
Ablative	aliis	aliis	aliis

Note:

In place of alius in the gen sing. **alterius** is often used

idem eadem idem the same

singular

Nominative	idem	eadem	idem
Accusative	eundem	eandem	idem
Genitive	eiusdem	eiusdem	eiusdem
Dative	eidem	eidem	eidem
Ablative	eodem	eadem	eodem

plural

Nominative	eidem	eaedem	eadem
Accusative	eosdem	easdem	eadem
Genitive	eorundem	earundem	eorundem
Dative	eisdem	eisdem	eisdem
Ablative	eisdem	eisdem	eisdem

Pronouns

qui quae quod   **who which**

singular

Nominative	qui	quae	quod
Accusative	quem	quam	quod
Genitive	cuius	cuius	cuius
Dative	cui	cui	cui
Ablative	quo	qua	quo

plural

Nominative	qui	quae	quae
Accusative	quos	quas	quae
Genitive	quorum	quarum	quorum
Dative	quibus	quibus	quibus
Ablative	quibus	quibus	quibus

Nominative	ego	tu	nos	vos
Vocative	-	tu	-	vos
Accusative	me	te	nos	vos
Genitive	mei	tui	nostri / nostrum	vestri / vestrum
Dative	mihi	tibi	nobis	vobis
Ablative	me	te	nobis	vobis

Verbs

Active

	1	2	3	4	3½	irreg.
Present						
I	amo	moneo	rego	audio	capio	sum
You (sing.)	amas	mones	regis	audis	capis	es
He, she, it	amat	monet	regit	audit	capit	est
We	amamus	monemus	regimus	audimus	capimus	sumus
You (pl.)	amatis	monetis	regitis	auditis	capitis	estis
They	amant	monent	regunt	audiunt	capiunt	sunt
Future						
I	amabo	monebo	regam	audiam	capiam	ero
You (sing.)	amabis	monebis	reges	audies	capies	eris
He, she, it	amabit	monebit	reget	audiet	capiet	erit
We	amabimus	monebimus	regemus	audiemus	capiemus	erimus
You (pl.)	amabitis	monebitis	regetis	audietis	capietis	eritis
They	amabunt	monebunt	regent	audient	capient	erunt
Imperfect						
I	amabam	monebam	regebam	audiebam	capiebam	eram
You (sing.)	amabas	monebas	regebas	audiebas	capiebas	eras
He, she, it	amabat	monebat	regebat	audiebat	capiebat	erat
We	amabamus	monebamus	regebamus	audiebamus	capiebamus	eramus
You (pl.)	amabatis	monebatis	regebatis	audiebatis	capiebatis	eratis
They	amabant	monebant	regebant	audiebant	capiebant	erant
Perfect						
I	amavi	monui	rexi	audivi	cepi	fui
You (sing.)	amavisti	monuisti	rexisti	audivisti	cepisti	fuisti
He, she, it	amavit	monuit	rexit	audivit	cepit	fuit
We	amavimus	monuimus	reximus	audivimus	cepimus	fuimus
You (pl.)	amavistis	monuistis	rexistis	audivistis	cepistis	fuistis
They	amaverunt	monuerunt	rexerunt	audiverunt	ceperunt	fuerunt
Pluperfect						
I	amaveram	monueram	rexeram	audiveram	ceperam	fueram
you (sing.)	amaveras	monueras	rexeras	audiveras	ceperas	fueras
He, she, it	amaverat	monuerat	rexerat	audiverat	ceperat	fuerat
We	amaveramus	monueramus	rexeramus	audiveramus	ceperamus	fueramus
You (sing.)	amaveratis	monueratis	rexeratis	audiveratis	ceperatis	fueratis
They	amaverant	monuerant	rexerant	audiverant	ceperant	fuerant
Infinitive	amare	monēre	regĕre	audire	capĕre	esse
Imperatives						
Sing.	ama	mone	rege	audi	cape	es
Pl.	amate	monete	regite	audite	capite	este

Passive

	1	2	3	4	3½
Present	amor	moneor	regor	audior	capior
	amaris	moneris	regeris	audiris	caperis
	amatur	monetur	regitur	auditur	capitur
	amamur	monemur	regimur	audimur	capimur
	amamini	monemini	regimini	audimini	capimini
	amantur	monentur	reguntur	audiuntur	capiuntur
Imperfect	amabar	monebar	regebar	audiebar	capiebar
	amabaris	monebaris	regebaris	audiebaris	capiebaris
	amabatur	monebatur	regebatur	audiebatur	capiebatur
	amabamur	monebamur	regebamur	audiebamur	capiebamur
	amabamini	monebamini	regebamini	audiebamini	capiebamini
	amabantur	monebantur	regebantur	audiebantur	capiebantur
Future	amabor	monebor	regar	audiar	capiar
	amaberis	moneberis	regeris	audieris	capieris
	amabitur	monebitur	regetur	audietur	capietur
	amabimur	monebimur	regemur	audiemur	capiemur
	amabimini	monebimini	regemini	audiemini	capiemini
	amabuntur	monebuntur	regentur	audientur	capientur

volo I want	**present**	**imperfect**	**future**	**perfect**	**pluperfect**
	volo	volebam	volam	volui	volueram
	vis	volebas	voles	voluisti	volueras
	vult	volebat	volet	voluit	voluerat
	volumus	volebamus	volemus	voluimus	volueramus
	vultis	volebatis	voletis	voluistis	volueratis
	volunt	volebant	volent	voluerunt	voluerant

Infinitive velle

nolo I don't want	**present**	**imperfect**	**future**	**perfect**	**pluperfect**
	nolo	nolebam	nolam	nolui	nolueram
	non vis	nolebas	noles	noluisti	nolueras
	non vult	nolebat	nolet	noluit	noluerat
	nolumus	nolebamus	nolemus	noluimus	nolueramus
	non vultis	nolebatis	noletis	noluistis	nolueratis
	nolunt	nolebant	nolent	noluerunt	noluerant

Infinitive nolle

possum I am able	**Present**	**imperfect**	**future**	**perfect**	**pluperfect**
	possum	poteram	potero	potui	potueram
	potes	poteras	poteris	potuisti	potueras
	potest	poterat	poterit	potuit	potuerat
	possumus	poteramus	poterimus	potuimus	potueramus
	potestis	poteratis	poteritis	potuistis	potueratis
	possunt	poterant	poterunt	potuerunt	potuerant

Infinitive   posse

eo I go	present	imperfect	future	perfect	pluperfect
	eo	ibam	ibo	ii *or* ivi	ieram
	is	ibas	ibis	isti, ivisti	ieras
	it	ibat	ibit	iit, ivit	ierat
	imus	ibamus	ibimus	iimus, ivimus	ieramus
	itis	ibatis	ibitis	istis, ivistis	ieratis
	eunt	ibant	ibunt	ierunt, iverunt	ierant

Infinitive ire
Imperative **sing.** i **pl**. ite

fero   I carry
active	present	imperfect	future	perfect	pluperfect
	fero	ferebam	feram	tuli	tuleram
	fers	ferebas	feres	tulisti	tuleras
	fert	ferebat	feret	tulit	tulerat
	ferimus	ferebamus	feremus	tulimus	tuleramus
	fertis	ferebatis	feretis	tulistis	tuleratis
	ferunt	ferebant	ferent	tulerunt	tulerant

infinitive ferre
imperative sing. fer **pl.** ferte

passive	present	imperfect	future	perfect	pluperfect
	feror	ferebar	ferar	latus sum	latus eram
	ferris	ferebaris	fereris	latus es	latus eras
	fertur	ferebatur	feretur	latus est	latus erat
	ferimur	ferebamur	feremur	lati sumus	lati eramus
	ferimini	ferebamini	feremini	lati estis	lati eratis
	feruntur	ferebantur	ferentur	lati sunt	lati erant

Latin – English word list

Latin	English
a, ab *(+abl.)*	from, by
absum, abesse, afui	be away
accipio ere accepi acceptum3 ½	receive
ad *(+acc.)*	to, towards
adsum, adesse, adfui	be present
advenio 4	arrive
aedifico 1	build
ager -ri 2 m	field
agricola -ae 1 m	farmer
alius -a -ud	other
altus -a -um	high, deep
ambulo 1	walk
amicus -i 1 m	friend
amo 1	like, love
ancilla -ae 1 f	maid-servant
animal -is 3 n	animal
annus -i 2 m.	year
ante	before
antequam	before
appropinquo 1	approach
aqua -ae 1 f	water
arma -orum 2 n	weapons
audax -acis	bold
audio 4	hear, listen
aurum -i 2 n	gold
autem	but
auxilium -i 2 n	help
bellum -i 2 n	war
bene	well
bibo -ere bibi bibitum 3	drink
bonus -a -um	good
caelum -i 2 n	sky
canto 1	sing
capio -ere cepi captum 3 ½	take, capture
carus -a -um	dear
celer -is -e	swift, quick
celeriter	quickly
ceteri	others
cibus -i 2 m	food
circum	around
civis -is 3 c	citizen
clamo 1	shout
clamor -is 3 m	shout
clarus -a -um	famous, clear
cogo -ere coegi coactum 3	force
colligo -ere collegi collectum 3	collect
comes -itis 3 c	companion
coniunx -iugis 3 c	husband, wife
conspicio -ere -spexi -ctum 3 ½	catch sight of
constituo -ere -i -utum 3	decide
consumo -ere -mpsi -mptum 3	eat
contendo -ere contendi 3	hurry
contra *(+acc.)*	against
convenio 4	meet
copiae -arum 1 f	forces
corpus -oris 3 n	body
cras	tomorrow
credo ere credidi creditum 3 *(+dat.)*	believe, trust
crudelis -e	cruel
cum *(+abl.)*	with
cupio -ere cupivi cupitum 3½	want, desire
cur?	why
curro -ere cucurri cursum 3	run
custos -odis 3 c	guard
custodio -ire -ivi -itum 4	guard
de *(+abl.)*	down from, about
dea -ae 1 f	goddess
decem	ten
decimus -a -um	tenth
defendo -ere -defendi defensum 3	defend
deinde	then, next
deleo -ere delevi deletum 2	destroy
deus -i 2 m	god
dico -ere dixi dictum 3	say, tell
dies -ei 5 m.	day
difficilis -e	difficult
discedo -ere discessi discessum 3	depart
diu	for a long time
do -are dedi 1	give
domus -us 4 f.	house
dominus -i 2 m	master
dormio 4	sleep
duco -ere duxi ductum 3	lead
dum	while
duo duae	two
duodecim	twelve
duodeviginti	eighteen
dux ducis 3 c	leader
e *(+abl.)*	out of, from
effugio -ere effugi 3 ½	escape
ego	I
eo ire -ii or -ivi itum	go
equus -i 2 m	horse
erro 1	wander
et	and
et … et	both .. and
etiam	even, also
ex *(+abl.)*	out of, from
exeo exire exii exitum	go out
exspecto 1	wait for
facilis -e	easy
facio -ere feci factum 3½	do, make
felix -icis	happy, lucky
femina -ae 1 f	woman
fero ferre tuli latum	bring, carry
fessus -a -um	tired
festino 1	hurry
fides -ei 5 f.	faith
filia -ae 1 f	daughter
filius -i 2 m	son
flumen -inis 3 n	river
forte	by chance
fortis -e	brave
fortiter	bravely
frater -ris 3 m	brother
frustra	In vain
fugio -ere fugi 3½	flee
fui	see sum
gens -tis 3 f	race, tribe
gero -ere gessi gestum 3	do, wear
gladius -i 2 m	sword
Graecus -a -um	Greek
habeo -ere habui habitum 2	have
habito 1	live

hasta -ae 1 f	spear	mora -ae 1 f	delay
heri	yesterday	mors mortis 3 f	death
hic	here	mortuus -a -um	dead
hic haec hoc	this; he, she, it	moveo -ere movi motum 2	move
hodie	today	mox	soon
homo -inis 3 c	man	mulier mulieris 3 f	woman
hora -ae 1 f	hour	multus -a -um	much, many
hostis -is 3 c	enemy pl.	murus -i 2 m	wall
iacio -ere ieci iactum 3½	throw	nam	for
iam	now, already	narro 1	tell
ibi	there	nauta -ae 1 m	sailor
idem eadem idem	same	navigo 1	sail
igitur	therefore	navis -is 3 f	ship
ille, illa, illud	that; he, she, it	-ne?	question
impero 1 (+dat.)	order	nec ... nec	neither ...nor
in (+abl.)	in, on	neco 1	kill
in (+acc.)	into	nemo neminis	nobody
incola -ae 1 c	inhabitant	neque ... neque	neither ... nor
ineo inire inii initum	go in	nihil	nothing
ingens -tis	huge	nobilis -e	noble
insula -ae 1 f	island	noli / nolite	do not!
inter (+acc.)	between, among	nolo nolle nolui	not want
interea	meanwhile	nomen nominis 3 n	name
interficio -ere -feci -fectum 3½	kill	non	not
intro 1	enter	nonne	surely?
invenio -ire inveni inventum 4	find	nonus -a -um	ninth
ira -ae 1 f	anger	nos	we, us
iratus -a -um	angry	noster -ra -rum	our
is ea id	that; he, she, it	notus -a -um	well-known
ipse -a -um	himself	novem	nine
Italia -ae	Italy	novus -a -um	new
itaque	therefore	nox noctis 3 f	night
iter itineris 3 n	journey	num?	surely not?
iterum	again	numquam	never
iubeo -ere iussi iussum 2	order	nunc	now
iuvenis iuvenis 3 c	young person	nuntius -i 2 m	messenger
iuvo 1	help	o	o!
labor -is 3 m	task, work	occido -ere occidi occisum 3	kill
laboro 1	work	occupo 1	seize
laetus a um	happy	octavus -a -um	eighth
laudo 1	praise	octo	eight
lego -ere legi lectum 3	read, choose	olim	once u. a time
liber -ri 2 m	book	omnis -e	every, all, whole
libero 1	free	oppidum -i 2 n	town
locus -i 2 m	place	oppugno 1	attack
longus -a -um	long	optimus -a -um	best
ludo -ere lusi lusum 3	play	opus operis 3 n	task, work
lux lucis 3 f	light	ostendo -ere ostendi ostentum 3	show
magister -ri 2 m	master	paene	scarcely, hardly
magnopere	greatly	parens -tis 3 c	parent
magnus -a -um	big, great	paro 1	prepare
malus -a -um	bad	parvus -a -um	small, little
maneo -ere mansi mansum 2	remain, stay	pater patris 3 m	father
mare maris 3 n	sea	patria -ae 1 f	fatherland
mater matris 3 f	mother	pauci	few
me	me	pecunia -ae 1 f	money
medius -a -um	middle	peior peius	worse
melior melius	better	pello -ere pepuli pulsum 3	drive
meus -a -um	my	per (+acc.)	through
miles militis 3 c	soldier	periculum -i 2 n	danger
miser -a -um	sad	persuadeo -ere persuasi 2	persuade
mitto -ere misi missum 3	send	perterritus -a –um	terrified
moneo -ere monui monitum 2	warn, advise	pessimus -a –um	worst
mons montis 3 m	mountain	peto ere petivi petitum 3	look for, attack

poeta -ae 1 m	poet	sine	without
pono -ere posui positum 3	put	socius -i 2 m	ally
porto 1	carry	solus -a -um	alone
possum posse potui	be able	somnus -i 3 m	sleep
post	after	soror sororis 3 f	sister
postea	afterwards	specto 1	watch
postquam	after	spes -ei 5 f	hope
praemium i 2 n.	reward, prize	statim	immediately
primus -a -um	first	sto -are steti statum 1	stand
princeps principis 3 m	chief	sub (+abl.)	under
pro	Instead of	subito	suddenly
proelium -i 2 n	battle	sum, esse, fui	be
prope	near	super (+acc.)	over
propter (+acc.)	on account of	superbus -a -um	proud, arrogant
puella -ae 1 f	girl	supero 1	overcome
puer -i 2 m	boy	suus -a -um	his, her, its
pugno 1	fight	tamen	however
pulcher -ra -rum	beautiful	tandem	at last
punio 4	punish	te	you
quam	than	tempestas tempestatis 3 f	storm
quamquam	although	templum -i 2 n	temple
quartus -a -um	fourth	teneo -ere tenui tentum2	hold
quattuor	four	terra -ae 1 f	land, earth
quattuordecim	fourteen	terreo -ere terrui territum 2	frighten
-que	and	tertius -a -um	third
qui quae quod	who,which	timeo -ere timui 2	fear
quid?	what?	totus -a -um	whole, all
quinque	five	trado -ere tradidi traditum 3	hand over
quintus -a -um	fifth	trans (+acc.)	across
quis?	who?	transeo -ire transii transitum	go across
quod	because	tredecim	thirteen
quoque	also	tres	three
redeo redire redii reditum	go back	tristis -e	sad
reduco -ere reduxi reductum3	lead back	tu	you
regina -ae I f	queen	tum	then
rego -ere rexi rectum3	rule	turba -ae 1 f	crowd
res -ei 5 f.	thing, matter	tutus -a -um	safe
respondeo -ere respondi responsum2	reply	tuus -a -um	your
rex regis 3 m	king	ubi	when
rideo -ere risi risum 2	laugh	ubi?	where?
rogo 1	ask	unda -ae 1 f	wave
Romanus -a -um	Roman	undeviginti	nineteen
ruo -ere rui rutum 3	rush	unus -a -um	one
sacer -ra -rum	scared	urbs urbis 3 f	city
saepe	often	uxor uxoris 3 f	wife
saevus -a -um	savage	validus -a -um	strong
sagitta -ae 1 f	arrow	venio 4	come
saluto 1	greet	ventus -i 2 m	wind
sapiens -tis	wise	verbum -i 2 n	word
scribo -ere scripsi scriptum 3	write	vester -ra -rum	your
scutum -i 2 n	shield	via -ae 1 f	road, street
secundus -a -um	second	video -ere vidi visum 2	see
sed	but	viginti	twenty
sedecim	sixteen	villa -ae 1 f	country-house
semper	always	vinco -ere vici victum3	conquer
senex senis 3 m	old man	vinum -i 2 n	wine
septem	seven	vir -i 2 m	man
septendecim	seventeen	virtus virtutis 3 f	courage
septimus -a -um	seventh	voco 1	call
servo 1	save	volo velle volui	want
servus -i 2 m	slave	vos	you
sex	six	vox vocis 3 f	voice
sextus -a -um	sixth	vulnero 1	wound
sic	thus	vulnus vulneris 3 n	wound

English – Latin word list

abandon	relinquo -ere reliqui relictum 3		body	corpus -oris 3 n
about	de *(+abl.)*		bold	audax -acis
across	trans *(+acc.)*		book	liber -ri 2 m
advance	progredior -i progressus 3½		both .. and	et … et
advise	moneo -ere monui monitum 2		boy	puer -i 2 m
affair	res, rei 5		brave	fortis -e
after	post *(+acc.)*		bravely	fortiter
after	postquam		bright	clarus -a -um
afterwards	postea		bring	fero ferre tuli latum
again	iterum		brother	frater -ris 3 m
against	contra *(+acc.)*		build	aedifico 1
alive	vivus -a -um		but	autem
all	omnis -e		but	sed
ally	socius -i 2 m		by	a, ab *(+abl.)*
almost	paene		by chance	forte
alone	solus -a -um		call	voco 1
already	iam		call together	convoco 1
also	quoque		can	possum posse potui
although	quamquam		capture	capio -ere cepi captum 3 ½
always	semper		carry	porto 1
among	inter *(+acc.)*		catch sight of	conspicio -ere -spexi -spectum 3 ½
and	et, -que		charge	ruo ruere rui rutum 3
and so	itaque		chieftain	princeps principis 3
anger	ira -ae 1 f		choose	lego -ere legi 3
angry	iratus -a -um		citizen	civis -is 3 c
animal	animal -is 3 n		city	urbs urbis 3 f
announce	nuntio 1		clear	clarus -a -um
answer	respondeo -ere respondi responsum		collect	colligo -ere collegi collectum 3
approach	appropinquo 1		come	venio 4
arms	arma armorum 2 n pl		companion	comes -itis 3 c
army	exercitus -us 4 m		conquer	vinco -ere vici victum 3
around	circum *(+acc.)*		courage	virtus virtutis 3 f
arrive	advenio 4		cross	transeo -ire transii transitum
arrogant	superbus -a -um		crowd	turba -ae 1 f
arrow	sagitta -ae 1 f		cruel	crudelis -e
ask	rogo 1		cry	fleo ere flevi 2
at last	tandem		danger	periculum -i 2 n
attack	oppugno 1		daring	audax audacis
bad	malus -a -um		daughter	filia -ae 1 f
battle	proelium -i 2 n		day	dies diei 5 m
be	sum, esse, fui		dead	mortuus -a -um
be able	possum posse potui		dear	carus -a -um
be afraid of	timeo -ere timui 2		death	mors mortis 3 f
be away	absum, abesse, afui		decide	constituo -ere -i -tum 3
be present	adsum, adesse, adfui		deep	altus -a –um
be wrong	erro 1		defeat	vinco -ere vici victum 3
beat	vinco -ere vici victum 3		defend	defendo -ere -i defensum3
beautiful	pulcher -ra -rum		delay	mora -ae 1 f
because	quod		depart	discedo -ere discessi discessum 3
before	ante *(+acc.)*		desire	cupio -ere cupivi cupitum 3½
before	antequam		destroy	deleo -ere delevi deletum2
believe	credo ere credidi 3 *(+dat.)*		die	morior mori mortuus 3½
best	optimus -a -um		difficult	difficilis -e
better	melior melius		dinner	cena -ae 1
between	inter *(+acc.)*		do	facio -ere feci factum 3½
big	magnus -a -um		do not!	noli / nolite
			do, make	facio -ere feci factum 3 ½
			do, wear	gero -ere gessi gestum 3

79

down from	de *(+abl.)*	guard n	custos custodis 3 c
drink	bibo -ere bibi bibitum3	guard v	custodio 4
drive	pello -ere pepuli pulsum 3	hand over	trado -ere tradidi traditum3
earth	terra -ae 1 f	handsome	pulcher pulchra pulchrum
easy	facilis -e	happy	laetus -a -um
eat	consumo -ere -mpsi -mptum3	harbour	portus -us 4 m
eight	octo	have	habeo -ere habui habitum 2
eighteen	duodeviginti	hear	audio 4
eighth	octavus -a -um	he	is, hic, ille
encourage	hortor -ari hortatus 1	help n	auxilium -i 2 n
enemy pl.	hostis -is 3 c	help v	iuvo -are iuvi iutum 1
enter	intro 1	her	suus -a -um
escape	effugio -ere effugi 3 ½	herself	se
even, also	etiam	here	hic
every	omnis -e	high	altus -a -um
everyone	omnes	his	suus -a -um
faith	fides -ei 5 f	hold	teneo -ere tenui tentum 2
famous	clarus -a -um	home	domus -us 4 f
farmer	agricola -ae 1 m	homeland	patria -ae 1
father	pater patris 3 m	hope n	spes spei 5 f
fatherland	patria -ae 1 f	horse	equus -i 2 m
fear	timeo -ere timui 2	hour	hora -ae 1 f
few	pauci	house	domus -us 4 f
field	ager -ri 2 m	however	tamen
fifth	quintus -a -um	huge	ingens -tis
fight	pugno 1	hurry	festino 1
find	invenio -ire inveni 4	husband	coniunx -iugis 3 c
first	primus -a -um	I	ego
five	quinque	immediately	statim
flee	fugio -ere fugi 3 ½	in	in *(+abl.)*
follow	sequor -i secutus 3	in vain	frustra
food	cibus -i 2 m	inhabitant	incola -ae 1 c
for	nam	instead of	pro
for a long time	diu	into	in *(+acc.)*
force	cogo -ere coegi coactum 3	island	insula -ae 1 f
forces	copiae -arum 1 f	Italy	Italia -ae
fortunate	felix felicis	its	suus -a -um
four	quattuor	javelin	telum -i 2 n
fourteen	quattuordecim	journey	iter itineris 3 n
fourth	quartus -a -um	kill	neco 1
free	libero 1	kill	occido -ere occidi occisum3
friend	amicus -i 1 m	kill	interficio -ere -feci -fectum 3½
frighten	terreo -ere terrui territum 2	king	rex regis 3 m
from	a, ab *(+abl.)*	know	scio -ere scivi scitum 4
general	dux ducis 3 m	land	terra -ae 1 f
gift	donum -i 2 n	later	postea
girl	puella -ae 1 f	laugh	rideo -ere risi 2
give	do -are dedi datum1	lead	duco -ere duxi ductum3
go	eo ire ii *or* ivi itum	lead back	reduco -ere reduxi reductum3
go across	transeo -ire -ii transitum	leader	dux ducis 3 m
go back	redeo redire redii reditum	leave (depart)	discedo -ere discessi discessum 3
go forward	progredior -i progressus 3½	leave(behind)	relinquo -ere reliqui relictum 3
go in	ineo inire inii initum	leave (go out)	egredior -i egressus 3½
go out	exeo exire exii exitum	light	lux lucis 3 f
go towards	adeo adire adii aditum	like	amo 1
god	deus -i 2 m	listen	audio 4
goddess	dea -ae 1 f	little	parvus -a -um
gold	aurum -i 2 n	live	habito 1
good	bonus -a -um	long	longus -a -um
great	magnus -a -um	look at	specto 1
greatly	magnopere	look for	peto -ere petivi petitum
Greek	Graecus -a -um	loud	magnus -a -um
greet	saluto 1	love	amo 1

lucky	felix -icis	proud	superbus -a -um
maid-servant	ancilla -ae 1 f	punish	punio 4
make	facio -ere feci factum 3½	pupil	discipulus -i 2 m
man	homo -inis 3 m	put	pono -ere posui positum 3
man	vir -i 2 m	queen	regina -ae I f
many	multi -ae -a	question	-ne?
march	contendo -ere contendi 3	quick	celer -is -e
master	dominus -i 2 m	quickly	celeriter
master (sch)	magister -ri 2 m	race	gens gentis 3 f
me	me	read	lego -ere legi lectum 3
meanwhile	interea	receive	accipio -ere accepi acceptum3 ½
meet	convenio 4	remain	maneo -ere mansi mansum 2
messenger	nuntius -i 2 m	reply	respondeo -ere -i responsum 2
middle	medius -a -um	return	redeo redire redii reditum
money	pecunia -ae 1 f	river	flumen -inis 3 n
mother	mater matris 3 f	road	via -ae 1 f
mountain	mons montis 3 m	Roman	Romanus -a -um
move	moveo -ere movi motum 2	rule	rego -ere rexi 3
much	multus -a -um	run	curro -ere cucurri cursum 3
my	meus -a -um	rush	ruo -ere rui rutum 3
name	nomen nominis 3 n	sacred	sacaer -ra -rum
near	prope (+acc.)	sad	miser -a -um
never	numquam	sad	tristis -e
new	novus -a -um	safe	tutus -a –um
next	deinde	sail	navigo 1
night	nox noctis 3 f	sailor	nauta -ae 1 m
nine	novem	savage	saevus -a -um
nineteen	undeviginti	save	servo 1
ninth	nonus -a -um	say	dico -ere dixi dictum 3
noble	nobilis -e	scared	sacer -ra -rum
nobody	nemo neminis	sea	mare maris 3 n
nor	nec, neque	second	secundus -a -um
not	non	see	video -ere vidi visum2
not know	nescio -ire nescivi nescitum 4	seek	peto -ere petivi petitum 3
not want	nollo nolle nolui	seize	occupo 1
nothing	nihil	self	Ipse ipsa ipsum
now	nunc	send	mitto -ere misi missum 3
now	iam, nunc	set out	proficiscor -i profectus 3
o!	o	seven	septem
often	saepe	seventeen	septendecim
old man	senex senis 3 m	seventh	septimus -a -um
on account of	propter (+acc.)	she	illa, ea, haec
once u. a time	olim	shield	scutum -i 2 n
one	unus -a -um	ship	navis -is 3 f
order	iubeo -ere iussi iussum 2	shout	clamo 1
other	alius alia aliud	shout	clamor -is 3 m
others	ceteri	show	ostendo ere -i ostentum 3
our	noster -ra -rum	sing	canto 1
out of	e, ex (+abl.)	sister	soror sororis 3 f
over	super (+acc.)	sit	sedeo -ere sedi sessum 2
overcome	supero 1	six	sex
parent	parens -tis 3 c	sixteen	sedecim
part	pars partis 3 f	sixth	sextus -a -um
perish	pereo perire perii peritum	sky	caelum -i 2 n
person	homo hominis 3 m/f	slave	servus -i 2 m
persuade	persuadeo -ere -suasi -suasum 2	sleep	dormio 4
place	locus -i 2 m	slowly	lente
play	ludo - ere lusi lusum 3	small	parvus -a -um
poet	poeta -ae 1 m	soldier	miles militis 3 c
praise	laudo 1	son	filius -i 2 m
prepare	paro 1	soon	mox
prize	praemium -i 2 n	speak	loquor -i locutus 3
promise	fides -ei 5	spear	hasta -ae 1 f, telum -i 2 n
		stand	sto -are steti statum1

stay	maneo -ere mansi mansum 2	want	cupio -ere cupivi cupitum3 ½
storm	tempestas tempestatis 3 f	war	bellum -i 2 n
street	via -ae 1 f	warn	moneo -ere monui monitum2
strong	validus -a -um	watch	specto 1
suddenly	subito	water	aqua -ae 1 f
suffer	patior pati passus 3½	wave	unda -ae 1 f
surely not?	num?	we, us	nos
surely?	nonne	weapons	arma -orum 2 n pl
sword	gladius -i 2 m	well	bene
take	capio -ere cepi captum 3 ½	well-known	notus -a -um
task	opus operis 3 n.	what?	quid?
teacher	magister -ri 2	when	ubi
tell	narro 1	where?	ubi?
temple	templum -i 2 n	while	dum
ten	decem	who?	quis?
tenth	decimus -a -um	why	cur?
terrified	perterritus -a -um	wicked	malus -a -um
than	quam	wife	uxor uxoris 3 f
that	ille illa illud	wind	ventus -i 2 m
the rest of	ceteri -ae -a	wine	vinum -i 2 n
their (own)	suus -a -um	wife	uxor -is 3 f
themselves	se	wise	sapiens sapientis
then	deinde	with	cum (+abl.)
there	Ibi	without	sine (+abl.)
therefore	igitur	woman	femina -ae 1 f
the same	idem eadem idem	woman	mulier mulieris 3 f
these	hi hae haec	word	verbum -i 2 n
thing	res rei 5 f	work n	labor laboris 3 m
third	tertius -a -um	work v	laboro 1
thirteen	tredecim	worse	peior peius
this	hic haec hoc	worst	pessimus -a -um
those	illi illae illa	wound	vulnus vulneris 3 n
three	tres tria	wound	vulnero 1
through	per (+acc.)	wound	vulnus vulneris 3 n
throw	iacio -ere ieci iactum3 ½	wretched	miser -a -um
thus	sic	write	scribo -ere scripsi scriptum3
tired	fessus -a -um	year	annus -i 2 m
to	ad (+acc.)	yesterday	heri
today	hodie	you	tu (nom. sing)
tomorrow	cras	you	te (acc. sing.)
towards	ad (+acc.)	you	vos pl.
town	oppidum -i 2 n	young person	iuvenis iuvenis 3 c
tribe	gens gentis 3 f	your	tuus -a -um
troops	copiae copiarum 1 f pl.	your	vester -ra -rum
trust	credo -ere credidi creditum 3		
try	conor -ari conatus 1		
twelve	duodecim		
twenty	viginti		
two	duo duae		
under	sub (+abl.)		
vain, in	frustra		
villa	villa -ae I f		
voice	vox vocis 3 f		
wait for	expecto 1		
walk	ambulo 1		
wall	murus -i 2 m		
wander	erro 1		